First Nations
and the
Canadian
State

First Nations and the Canadian State

In Search of Coexistence

Alan C. Cairns

2002 Kenneth R. MacGregor Lecturer

Institute of Intergovernmental Relations
School of Policy Studies, Queen's University

Library and Archives Canada Cataloguing in Publication

Cairns, Alan C.
    First Nations and the Canadian state : in search of coexistence / Alan C. Cairns.

Includes bibliographical references.
ISBN 1-55339-014-8

    1. Native peoples—Canada. 2. Native peoples—Canada—Government relations.
3. Native peoples—Legal status, laws, etc.—Canada. I. Queen's University (Kingston, Ont.).
Institute of Intergovernmental Relations II. Title.

E92.C223 2005   323.1197'071   C2005-904050-5

The Institute of Intergovernmental Relations

The Institute is the only organization in Canada whose mandate is solely to promote research and communication on the challenges facing the federal system.

Current research interests include fiscal federalism, the social union, health policy, the reform of federal political institutions and the machinery of federal-provincial relations, Canadian federalism and the global economy, and comparative federalism.

The Institute pursues these objectives through research conducted by its own staff and other scholars, through its publication program, and through seminars and conferences.

The Institute links academics and practitioners of federalism in federal and provincial governments and the private sector.

The Institute of Intergovernmental Relations receives ongoing financial support from the J.A. Corry Memorial Endowment Fund, the Royal Bank of Canada Endowment Fund, the Government of Canada, and the Government of Ontario. We are grateful for this support which enables the Institute to sustain its extensive program of research, publication, and related activities.

L'Institut des relations intergouvernementales

L'Institut est le seul organisme canadien à se consacrer exclusivement à la recherche et aux échanges sur les questions du fédéralisme.

Les priorités de recherche de l'Institut portent présentement sur le fédéralisme fiscal, l'union sociale, la santé, la modification éventuelle des institutions politiques fédérales, les mécanismes de relations fédérales-provinciales, le fédéralisme canadien au regard de l'économie mondiale et le fédéralisme comparatif.

L'Institut réalise ses objectifs par le biais de recherches effectuées par son personnel et par des chercheurs de l'Université Queen's et d'ailleurs, de même que par des congrès et des colloques.

L'Institut sert comme lien entre les universitaires, les fonctionnaires fédéraux et provinciaux et le secteur privé.

L'Institut des relations intergouvernementales reçoit l'appui financier du J.A. Corry Memorial Endowment Fund, de la Fondation de la Banque Royale du Canada, du gouvernement du Canada et du gouvernement de l'Ontario. Nous les remercions de cet appui qui permet à l'Institut de poursuivre son vaste programme de recherche et de publication ainsi que ses activités connexes.

The need to bring ... Aboriginal peoples into our national consciousness, to deal fairly and equitably with them, to reconcile them as part of the Canadian mainstream and to deal with their problems, [is] likely the most important public policy issue of the 21st century.

John Crosbie, former Conservative cabinet minister (Crosbie 2003).

CONTENTS

FOREWORD

Professor Alan Cairns delivered a public address on "First Nations and the Canadian State: In Search of Co-Existence" as the Kenneth R. MacGregor Lecturer in Intergovernmental Relations in October 2002. This publication is the revised and much expanded text of that presentation.

Alan Cairns has long been one of Canada's pre-eminent scholars and a distinguished contributor to the literature on federalism and issues surrounding Aboriginal development and governance. A graduate of the University of Toronto and Oxford, Professor Cairns was formerly a Research Director of the Royal Commission on the Economic Union and Development Prospects for Canada, Professor Emeritus of the University of British Columbia and currently Adjunct Professor of Political Science at the University of Waterloo. His analyses of constitutional politics and of the institutions and dynamics of Canadian federalism have been widely published. He has influenced students of federalism in this country in the way they view the Canadian constitution.

This is the second time Professor Cairns has delivered the MacGregor Lecture. As the 1987 MacGregor Lecturer, he examined the role of the constitution in Canadian society, and how constitutional reform since 1982 affected citizens and governments alike and transformed the nature of political debate in Canada. In this volume, Professor Cairns extends some of the previous scholarship surrounding the concept of "citizens-plus." In particular, he has explored some of the practical macro-policy steps that may be necessary in order to better bridge the gaps between Aboriginal and non-Aboriginal Canadians. His ideas, in this regard, merit careful public deliberation in the period ahead.

Queen's University established the MacGregor Lectureship in order to bring to the campus from time to time a prominent public figure or scholar who can make an important contribution to the understanding or practice of federalism, intergovernmental relations or related matters in Canada or other countries. The lectureship is funded by an endowment in honour of Kenneth R. MacGregor who had a distinguished career in the field of insurance, including its intergovernmental complexities, in particular as the federal Superintendent of Insurance (1953 to 1964), and President of Mutual Life Assurance of Canada (1964 to 1973). He was also a member of the Queen's University Board of Trustees.

Other previous MacGregor Lecturers have included Robert Stanfield, Peter Lougheed, Allan Blakeney, Albert Breton, Gordon Robertson, Daniel Elazar, Roger Gibbins and Richard Simeon.

The Institute of Intergovernmental Relations is delighted to be able to publish this very important contribution to the study of federalism and intergovernmental relations in Canada.

Harvey Lazar
Director, Institute of
Intergovernmental Relations
June 2005

ACKNOWLEDGEMENTS

I wish to thank the Institute of Intergovernmental Relations and the Canadian Network of Federalism Studies for sponsoring this lecture, and also Mutual Life of Canada and Friends of Kenneth MacGregor for funding support. I owe special thanks to Harvey Lazar, Director of the Institute of Intergovernmental Relations, for inviting me.

This is my second MacGregor opportunity. I gave a series of three MacGregor lectures in 1987, which led to *Charter versus Federalism* in 1992 (Cairns 1992a).

RÉSUMÉ

Depuis près de 50 ans, principalement en raison du nationalisme québécois, les Canadiens ont entrepris un processus quasi-ininterrompu d'introspection constitutionnelle en quête des moyens institutionnels susceptibles de leur procurer un sentiment d'unité au sein d'une fédération à la fois très étendue et très diversifiée. Mettre les Premières nations et autres peuples autochtones à l'ordre du jour constitutionnel a donné une nouvelle dimension et prédominance aux questions de la citoyenneté canadienne et de l'unité nationale. Nous nous trouvons donc au milieu d'un conflit entre un État canadien démocratique qui s'occupe d'immigration, laquelle constitue une exigence fonctionnelle de sa capacité à régner efficacement, et un peuple autochtone nationaliste frustré par les contraintes de ce projet de développement de pays. Dans cette dissertation, Alan Cairns trace le portrait de cette lutte et suggère une manière de penser qui pourrait nous mener à un terrain d'entente viable.

Cette dissertation illustre essentiellement une vision scientifique et politique qui permettrait aux peuples autochtones et non autochtones de partager la moitié d'un continent. Cette vision s'appuie sur quatre états de faits particuliers. Le premier est celui du mouvement anti-colonial mondial des peuples autochtones dans les sociétés colonisées, perçu comme étant la deuxième phase de l'anti-colonialisme qui a fait suite aux populaires mouvements d'indépendance du Tiers-Monde. Le deuxième décrit diverses réalités autochtones au Canada telles que la population autochtone vivant en milieu urbain, le nombre élevé de mariages entre autochtones et non autochtones, la petite taille des communautés des Premières nations et le grand nombre de gens dont les ancêtres sont autochtones, mais qui ne s'identifient pas à ces derniers. Le troisième présente une étude sur l'aliénation constitutionnelle autochtone en ce qui à trait au Parlement, aux élections, au système fédéral (en particulier les provinces), à la Chartre et à la citoyenneté canadienne. Enfin, le quatrième et dernier état de fait tente, considérant les difficultés liées au statut d'autochtone, de faire la synthèse de deux perspectives plutôt contradictoires qui rallient l'unité nationale et la diversité multinationale, et qui sont toutes les deux associées au philosophe Charles Taylor. Dans ses commentaires intitulés « A Recipe for Living Together », le professeur Cairns fait une série de recommandations pratiques sur la manière dont les autochtones et les autres Canadiens pourraient se bâtir un avenir commun.

FIRST NATIONS AND THE CANADIAN STATE
IN SEARCH OF COEXISTENCE

INTRODUCTION

Before this essay gets underway, a disciplinary caution is appropriate to inform the listener (now reader) that different academic disciplines bring different perspectives to the Aboriginal policy area. Contemporary Aboriginal policy discussion in Canada is heavily influenced by the academic legal community, whose prominence is a natural response to the extensive judicialization of this policy area. The goal of legal theorists (Patrick Macklem 2001; Kent McNeil 2001*a, b, c*; Brad Morse 1999*a, b*) is to find and, if possible, enlarge the constitutional space available for the flourishing of First Nations peoples and governments. Political theorists (Joe Carens 2000; Will Kymlicka 1995, 1998; Charles Taylor 1999; Jim Tully 1999) are also influential in framing the intellectual debate. Historians are relevant in the court room when divergent pasts confront each other (J.R. Miller 2004; Arthur J. Ray 2000, with Jim Miller and Frank Tough),[1] and urban geographers and sociologists will acquire greater visibility as urban issues become increasingly important (Carol LaPrairie 1995; David Newhouse and Evelyn Peters 2003*a*).[2] Although John Richards (2004; Richards and Vining 2003, 2004) is an exception, economics has not played the kind of role that urban Aboriginal poverty, and the hopes for reserve-based economic development, suggest.[3] Remarkably, anthropology, formerly the lead discipline in the study of Aboriginal peoples, has clearly lost its dominance. (See, however, Noel Dyck 1991 and the late Sally Weaver 1981.)

Another disciplinary development of note is the crucial distinction between the growing community of Aboriginal scholars — (Taiaiake Alfred 1999; Daniel Beavon and Martin Cooke 2003; John Borrows 2001; Paul Chartrand 1999; Joyce Green 1993; James [sakej] Youngblood Henderson 2000, with

Marjorie L. Benson and Isobel M. Findlay; Kiera Ladner 2003*a,b*; Patricia Monture-Angus 1995; David Newhouse 2003; Mary Jane Norris and Stewart Clatworthy 2003; Mary Ellen Turpel 1989/90) — and their non-Aboriginal counterparts, who previously monopolized research on Aboriginal policy issues. Their university presence and visibility are reinforced by the emergence of Departments of Native Studies across the country. Aboriginal scholars bring to this subject an existential empathy that non-Aboriginal scholars cannot command. Occasionally, it is suggested that true knowledge/understanding of Aboriginal issues is unavailable to outsiders lacking lived experience.[4]

My own position is straightforward: the more disciplinary diversity the better. Disciplinary monopolies — even if only relative, and regardless of which discipline plays the lead role — always need supplementation by the divergent perspectives of other disciplines.[5] Moreover, the coexistence of Aboriginal and non-Aboriginal scholars within disciplines is a positive development, since it helps to overcome the historic hegemony of non-Aboriginal scholars from the majority society. An increase in the number of scholars of Métis and Inuit backgrounds would be welcome additions to the scholarly community addressing Métis and Inuit policy questions, subject areas that are relatively under-studied.

I write and speak as an older political scientist. I would like to say as an "elder," but it has been gently suggested that simply "old" is more appropriate. I place political science, especially if political theory is included, somewhat below legal analysis in terms of relative importance. As a political scientist, I am concerned with the overall viability of the constitutional order which emerges from the search for a rapprochement between First Nations, the Canadian state, and the non-Aboriginal majority population. I do not regard this concern as a capitulation to the status quo, but as a recognition of the inescapable reality that none of us has a blank slate on which we can write as we will.[6] A concern for constitutional viability and workability is an essential requirement of helpful policy-thinking.

This is a natural focus for a political scientist, especially a Canadian one, and more particularly a non-Aboriginal one. For nearly half a century, driven largely by Quebec nationalism, Canadians have engaged in an almost uninterrupted process of constitutional introspection, seeking answers to the question "Should we remain together as a people?" and if the answer is "yes," what rearrangements of our constitutional life and its institutional components are viable and appropriate? The emergence of First Nations and other Aboriginal peoples onto the public agenda has given the issue of our togetherness a new dimension and salience.

The combination of disciplinary rivalry, the disagreement over how we are to live together, the emergence of an Aboriginal scholarly community, the colonial background to contemporary debates, and the emotions that inevitably attend a policy focus in which nations and nationalism are central objects of analysis generate a policy discourse in which acrimony may overwhelm civility, or political criteria may stifle discussion.[7] I will try not to succumb to these pressures.

One final *obiter dictum*. I apologize for focusing largely on First Nations, and thus for not engaging in what would have been a valuable comparative analysis of all three incumbents of section 35 of the *Constitution Act, 1982* — Inuit and Métis as well as Indian, the three Aboriginal Peoples of Canada. I plead limitations of time, space, and human frailty, while admitting that aggregate Aboriginal data is occasionally used to supplement First Nations specific data, which is not always easily available.[8]

My purpose in the following pages is to offer a political science contribution to the discussion of how Aboriginal, especially Indian nations/peoples, and non-Aboriginal Canadians are to share half a continent. Four contexts are of special importance in grounding the discussion. The first is the global anti-colonial movement of indigenous peoples in settler societies. This has to be understood as the second stage of anti-colonialism following the successful Third World anti-colonial movements leading to independence. The second context is various indigenous realities in Canada, including the urban Aboriginal population, high rates of intermarriage, the small size of First Nation communities, and the large Aboriginal ancestry population which does not self-identify as Aboriginal. These foci verge on taboo status: delicate subjects which the cautious prefer to avoid. The third context comprises a survey of Aboriginal constitutional alienation with respect to Parliament, elections, the federal system (especially the provinces), the Charter, and Canadian citizenship. The fourth and final context examines the question "What is to be done?" through an attempted accommodation of two somewhat contradictory "big picture" choices, both associated with the Canadian philosopher Charles Taylor.

The picture that emerges in the following pages is exceedingly, a critic might say excessively, complex. I admit the former, but reject the latter. In a sense, the paper is a criticism of the grand simplifiers, in which camp I locate both the 1969 White Paper, and the 1996 Report of the Royal Commission on Aboriginal Peoples (RCAP). My complexity is a deliberate response to the simplifications of both big pictures. The former (White Paper) paternalistically assumed that Indian peoples were passive clay to be moulded into standard Canadians. The latter (RCAP) assumed that the multinational Canada it almost casually proposed could somehow be accommodated with little demur from the inhabitants of existing constitutional arrangements.

The reconciliation of the momentum of the centuries-old state form and the passions of indigenous nationalism still eludes us after half a century of effort since the extension of the franchise to status Indians in 1960. We are caught in a conflict between a *dirigiste* democratic Canadian state which "seeks to shape its people into some degree of unity...[a state which] is in the business of creating citizens as a functional requirement for its effective ruling capacity" (Cairns 2003*a*, 504), and indigenous nationalism frustrated by constraints that trap it within the borders of a relatively inflexible state. This essay seeks to outline the contours of that struggle and to suggest a manner of thinking that might move us in the direction of a viable middle ground.

My goal is both ambitious and limited: ambitious in the territory I seek to cover, and the macro-perspective frequently employed and limited in that my answer to "What is to be done?" is, in fact, tentative, even though it is forcefully argued. The debate about alternative futures is sufficiently complex that a healthy dose of modesty is an appropriate trait.

Two readers of the first version of this paper suggested that I should translate the general argument of its concluding sections into more specific recommendations as to how Aboriginal and other Canadians could more fruitfully live together. I have tried to do so in a Postscript: A Recipe for Living Together.

FROM AN IMPERIAL TO A POST-IMPERIAL ERA: THIRD WORLD TO FOURTH WORLD

Why is the issue of Aboriginal-state relations so difficult? The answer is located at the juncture of two powerful forces: the contemporary state form fashioned over centuries on the one hand, and on the other, indigenous nationalisms trapped in domestic settings that are less open to transformation than the international system was to the Third World nationalism that toppled empires. In the last half-century we have moved into the second stage of the global reconfiguration of peoples/nations/states and of the international system. The first stage saw the end of the overseas European empires that had controlled much of humanity. The world in which Europeans were, in Kiernan's apt phrase, *The Lords of Human Kind,* was coming to an end (Kiernan 1972). Within a few decades after World War II, the French, Belgian, Portuguese, British, and Dutch empires collapsed with a speed that almost no one had predicted. The German scholar Jurgen Habermas saw decolonization as one of the few positive events in what Robert Conquest referred to as "a ravaged century" (Habermas 2001, 45-48; Conquest 2000).

The second stage, the ending of internal empire, is now underway. Stage two is also a global movement, wherein indigenous peoples are drivn by a desire similar to that which previously inspired Nigerians, Indonesians, Algerians, and Vietnamese to struggle against colonial rule by imperial powers. Both stages are research areas of great complexity and very high emotions.[9] Although the stage-one ending of overseas empire has entered into our historical consciousness, and understandably tends to dwarf the local struggles of internal minority indigenous nations,[10] the latter's struggles should themselves be understood and located in the context of a global movement of peoples (in this case indigenous) seeking escape from marginalization and colonization in settler societies. The contemporary global movement of indigenous peoples, drawing on and inspired by its Third World predecessors in overseas colonies, informs the decolonization process in every locale where it is underway.

Although Third and Fourth World peoples were both subject to the hierarchy of imperialism, the latter were never treated as peoples/nations on the road to independence. In Canada, Indian peoples were placed outside the standard working of the majority's constitutional order, and governed in geographically discrete communities by superintendents who were the domestic counterparts of district officers in British colonial sub-Saharan Africa. The system of Indian reserves could be thought of as transitional appendages to the mainstream constitutional order, while the policy of assimilation — for which church-run residential schools were key instruments — eroded cultural diversity. In the context of Canadian domestic imperialism, therefore, the governing logic of the state was that indigenous difference was transitional: to be overcome by state pressure and inducements.

What is striking and far too infrequently noticed in this domestic imperial history is that, in traditional policy terms, the basic constitutional order was sacrosanct. Indians were either outside the constitutional order that applied to the majority — defined and treated as wards — or were subsequently to be fully within it as standard citizens, although their route to citizenship would differ from that travelled by other Canadians. Contemporary First Nations nationalism renders the traditional policy obsolete. It rejects both wardship and legislated inferiority as well as the disappearance of Indians into the majority society. These rejections mean that the institutional framework of the constitutional order can no longer be taken for granted, as it was from a traditional policy perspective.

Indian peoples have rejected both the historic practice of stigmatized exclusion and the historic assumption that it was to be ended by their assimilation and disappearance. In traditional policy terms, domestic empire and internal colonialism were to end by Indians, as individuals, entering the majority society and its unchanged constitutional order on the majority's terms. In the contemporary post-imperial era, empire is to end with the emergence of constitutionally recognized and protected self-governing First Nation communities in a transformed constitutional order. This is the novelty and challenge of the contemporary era.

Yesterday's stigmatized but presumably interim exclusion has to be transformed into a positive differential in relation to the constitutional order which is intended to endure. Contemporary First Nations nationalism pushes for major change in the direction of some version of a future multinational Canada. The traditional constitutional order accordingly is no longer a given. Of course, it has already been profoundly transformed by section 35(1) of the *Constitution Act, 1982* with its directive that: "The existing aboriginal and treaty rights of the aboriginal peoples of Canada are hereby recognized and affirmed," although the practical recognition of those rights remains unfinished business.

The source of Third World anti-colonial nationalism in yesterday's overseas colonies and in the contemporary Fourth World of indigenous minority nations is identical: the colonized status of subject peoples. Further, both Third and Fourth World nationalist movements took those in power by surprise, which suggests a very volatile policy area buffeted by passion.[11] Nevertheless, although the Fourth World response to internal colonialism builds on the earlier response to overseas colonialism of Third World peoples, the lessons of the latter lack immediate applicability to Fourth World conditions. This is beautifully illustrated in a newspaper account noting that the Haida Nation in British Columbia has filed a writ with the BC Supreme Court laying claim to all the lands in the Queen Charlotte Islands, plus resources in and under the sea. Haida President Guujaaw asserted that the Haida believe they are an independent nation and are owners of the land. However, "practical realities being what they are, the Haida, [he said], are willing to accept a 'lesser' designation of having aboriginal title to the land under Canadian law because 'there are other people living on the land now' … The alternative, to 'decolonize' Haida Gwaii as was done in Africa and Asia and turn the island into an independent nation, is not practical, he said" (Lee and McInnes 2002; see also Hume 2002; and *The Globe and Mail* 2002).

The Haida story can be generalized to other Aboriginal peoples living in Canada whose national ambitions are similarly frustrated by the fact that "other people," vastly superior in numbers, also live on the land. "Independent statehood," as Joseph Carens observes, "is not a realistic option for most aboriginal peoples" (Carens 2000, 179). Ovide Mercredi, former National Chief of the Assembly of First Nations, agrees: "With a population of fewer than one million, we know we cannot displace the alien government completely, and this is not our objective. The objective is to live together" (Mercredi and Turpel 1993, 198).

How to do so, however, remains in question. Indigenous peoples, settler majorities and their governments in democratic societies may agree on the desirability of winding down the internal empire, and yet disagree on the precise nature of its replacement. First Nations anti-colonial nationalism focuses on maximizing autonomy in a context in which they cannot escape from permanent minority status. The federal and provincial governments of the federal system, by contrast, are driven by the functional requirement that their people share some degree of civic togetherness sustained by reciprocal empathy.

THE DOMESTIC CONSEQUENCES OF GLOBAL REALITIES

The global overseas empires of European powers in Africa, Asia, and elsewhere helped sustain the historic Canadian Indian policy of wardship/assimilation. The pervasive set of assumptions that undergirded the overseas empire made domestic Indian policy in the imperial era appear to be part of the natural order. Conversely, the ending of global empire in the decades post-World War II removed support for domestic empire over indigenous peoples in Canada, Australia, and elsewhere. In Canada, for example, the 1960 extension of the franchise to status Indians, the 1969 White Paper and RCAP, in spite of the different assumptions and hopes that drove them, were all responses to the ongoing process of ending formal European hegemony over much of the world. As such, they were responses either to the achieved (Third World) or anticipated (Fourth World) triumph of anti-imperialism. In sum, the end of the British empire in India and elsewhere and the subsequent collapse of other European empires removed a crucial justification for the wardship status of Indian peoples in Canada. Wardship status, no longer part of the natural order, became an anachronism almost overnight.

The colonial nationalism which overthrew empires and the less ambitious internal indigenous nationalism in settler colonies now underway were and are similar responses to similar indignities. The most basic was the ultimate indignity of being placed under the paternal authority of others, ostensibly for one's own good. Indigenous peoples' control over their own future was removed. In both cases the non-indigenous rulers complacently assumed the justice of this usurpation. Overseas colonies were maintained under a system of tutelage. Internal indigenous minorities in settler colonies were defined and treated as wards. Both were subjected to the hegemony of European peoples, and to the disparagement of their cultures. In a famous phrase, Nehru spoke for both when he defined one of the nationalist goals as freedom "from contempt" (Perham 1970, 184).[12] Both Third and Fourth World nationalist movements have employed a common language of anti-colonialism as an instrument of mobilization.

Chris Tennant, in comparing the image of indigenous peoples in international institutions and in the international legal literature, documented an image reversal between two periods: 1945–58, still the imperial era, and 1971–93, a post-imperial world. In the first period, "assimilation and integration were unproblematically desirable objectives, and had clearly defined meanings in the context of an unquestioned background rhetoric of progress" (Tennant 1994, 29).[13] In the more recent period, by contrast, "the idea of a ladder of cultural evolution with indigenous peoples at the bottom of the ladder, is no longer acceptable" (ibid., 24). Paternalism and assimilation, accordingly, are in retreat, replaced by the thesis that "indigenous peoples should share in the common entitlements of the modern world: self-determination, full legal and political capacity, and the general right to choose and determine their own future" (ibid., 37-38). The transformation, which Tennant documents in the international arena, is duplicated in the Canadian domestic context, with some slippage in dates; a process clearly illustrated by the contrast between the assimilationist 1969 White Paper and the recognition of Aboriginal and treaty rights in the *Constitution Act, 1982*.

Canadians live, accordingly, in a post-imperial or post-colonial world, initially triggered and defined by a global redistribution of status in the international system, which then spilled over into the domestic arenas of settler states where it stimulated both indigenous nationalisms and a relative settler willingness to dismantle the institutions of domestic colonialism. Not surprisingly, similar trends emerge in western democratic societies open to the evolution of international opinion on the illegitimacy of internal colonialism. In a comparative analysis of indigenous peoples and the state in Canada, Australia, New Zealand, Denmark and Norway, Frances Abele notes the remarkable fact "not that the wronged [indigenous] group remembers and seeks redress, but that significant numbers in the dominant group wish to acknowledge the injustices and to work on recuperation and reparation" (Abele 2001, 145).

These brief observations remind us that we need to look outside our Canadian selves to understand the political challenges we face. Our domestic history is intertwined with a global history.[14] Indigenous peoples are aware that they are not alone. They gain psychological support from the possibility and hope that this time perhaps history is on their side.[15] The anti-colonialism of Fourth World indigenous peoples in settler societies draws sustenance from the prior success of formerly colonized Third World peoples in toppling European empires and reshaping the global map. Settler majorities understand at some level, although in some cases reluctantly, that their domestic world changed with the end of overseas empire in distant continents, and that hierarchy and paternalism, formerly taken for granted, are on the defensive. This psychological transformation is part of the pervasive backdrop to contemporary debates on decolonization.

As the international environment changes, the incentives and disincentives for various domestic policy choices are rearranged. The thinking of one generation can be repudiated by the successor generation. The missionary fervour that generated the 1969 White Paper is displaced a quarter of a century later by the no less passionate fervour of the 1996 Report of the Royal Commission on Aboriginal peoples — both driven by passion, but directed to antithetical goals. Such generational turnarounds are not uncommon: witness the transition from apartheid to Mandela in South Africa, and from the "cultural revolution" to the "capitalist road to socialism" in China. They are reminders that we discern the future darkly, and that while we must respond to the here and now, a certain modesty and appreciation of our fallibility are sentiments that will serve us well.

THE FOURTH WORLD IS NOT THE THIRD WORLD

Although Third and Fourth World nationalisms are linked phenomena, they are also distinct. While Fourth World nationalism draws inspiration from its Third World predecessor, it must confront a very different political environment which necessarily constrains the possibilities for choice and change. The version of nationalism that induced the British to leave India and the French to leave Senegal must be adapted to the different realities of the Fourth World. At a minimum, the Fourth World nationalist project must accommodate itself to an ongoing relationship with the majority population within the same state that was the historic agent of indigenous dispossession. This is true of Canada, the United States, Australia, and New Zealand but less so of

Mexico and some countries in South America. In the Third World, the imperial power formally departs; in the Fourth World what was the imperial majority remains behind, perhaps no longer imperial, but still the majority.

An overseas imperial power can pack up its flags and depart. Settler majorities, however, cannot scuttle and run as the Belgians did in the Congo. They remain behind as majorities. They have no distant home across the oceans to return to as had the imperial administrative class displaced by indigenization in tropical colonies. Most importantly, these settler communities are not suddenly relegated to minority status as was the case for minority settler communities in Kenya or Zimbabwe, whose previously privileged position derived not from their numbers, but from their linkage with the imperial presence in the heyday of overseas empire. In the Fourth World the settler community and its governments in what used to be called the "white dominions" in the then-British empire, must work out a *modus vivendi* within a shared political community with formerly colonized First Nations. This requirement of some version of non-hierarchical togetherness constrains both parties. It precludes the pursuit of the futures that an unconstrained non-Aboriginal majority might otherwise select. Simultaneously, the possible futures that First Nations can meaningfully pursue are limited by the ongoing majority presence. There is no vacated state for them to occupy and take over, no equivalent to what their Third World predecessors inherited. The more limited goal of carving out a space for one or more internal indigenous nations within the ongoing constitutional order of a particular state is a different task from that facing an autonomous, newly independent Third World state entering the international state system. Denied the goal of independence, the objectives of Fourth World anti-colonial nationalism accordingly cannot simply duplicate the objectives of their Third World predecessors. Fourth World nationalism has to be domesticated to the task of coexistence with the majority within the same polity.

The above noted difference needs underlining, for it tends to be blurred by the language of anti-colonial indigenous nationalism common in both Third and Fourth World settings. The Third World evolution from colony to nation was facilitated by a receptive international environment. The emerging nation had a ready-made international state system available to receive new players.[16] While the international system was dramatically transformed by the vast increase in the number of club members, it was nevertheless an accommodating system. Independence was a natural outcome for both the imperial power and the nationalism that confronted it. The imperial power could even applaud the arrival of an independence its armies might previously have resisted with the "after-the-fact" rhetorical consolation that its nation-building task was complete. For these and other reasons the formal ending of Third World overseas imperialism is easier for both parties than is the case for settler majorities and minority indigenous nations in Fourth World settings.[17] Post-colonialism in a Third World setting has a certain clarity not yet achieved in the anti-colonial struggles in the Fourth World. In fact, a similar degree of clarity in Fourth World conditions is inherently unattainable, since every available outcome is a compromise that requires some rapprochement between the successors of the former imperial majority and the formerly colonized indigenous peoples.[18] These populations have to live together within the same polity, a reality that will inevitably be experienced as a frustration from the nationalist indigenous perspective.

Successful Third World anti-colonial movements transformed the international system by changing the numbers and the composition of the players. Statehood gave voice to the new players, resulting in a transformed international conversation about the nature and norms of a post-colonial world. Hedley Bull's summary is apposite: Third World states "have overturned the old structure of international law and organization that once served to sanctify their subject status. The equal rights of non-western states to sovereignty, the rights of non-western peoples to self-determination, the rights of non-white races to equal treatment, non-western peoples to economic justice, and non-western cultures to dignity and autonomy" are embodied in "conventions having the force of law," although their implementation does not always follow, and their interpretation is often disputed (Bull 1984, 227).

The end of overseas empire not only rearranged the distribution of power and status in the international community, but undermined the ideologies that sustained the dominance of settler majorities over minority indigenous populations in Canada and elsewhere. Thus, much of Hedley Bull's report of a new international paradigm has a domestic counterpart. Ideologies which had justified wardship status for Indian peoples and marginalization for Inuit and Métis were dropped. The cultural assault on Indian practices such as the potlatch ended. Assimilation was no longer the official goal. Aboriginal and treaty rights in Canada received constitutional protection in 1982. Indigenous culture, no longer restricted to pre-contact behaviour, was redefined in terms of a modernizing Aboriginality. The non-Aboriginal monopoly of policy discussion of Aboriginal futures was ended. Most important, the permanent existence of distinct First Nations in Canada was assumed (see Weaver 1990, 12).

That permanent existence, however, is of internal nations whose attainable goal is not independence but the finding of constitutional space and culturally sensitive policies. The pursuit and attainment of these goals is conditioned by particular national settings. Although the anti-colonial language of nationalism is ubiquitous in Canada — it permeated the RCAP report, for example — independence, the logical antithesis to colonialism, is not an available option. This is the crucial tension, or the cruel reality, at the heart of indigenous nationalism in Canada. Fourth World indigenous nationalism can only be understood in the context of the prior break-up of the European powers that had controlled much of humanity. The end of overseas empire stimulated indigenous nationalism in settler colonies. That nationalism, however, can only be understood if the political realities in settler colonies are constantly distinguished from the very different realities that prevailed in overseas colonies. While the distinction is clear, working out its consequences, which is where we are now in Canada, is immensely difficult.

Although the transformed international climate has been a crucial factor informing policy thinking in Canada, its influence here and in other countries has been shaped by the distinctive national histories and constitutional arrangements, and the varying size of the indigenous populations it has confronted. Three such factors that have been crucial in the Canadian context are discussed in the next section.[19]

THREE CRUCIAL DEMOGRAPHIC REALITIES FOR CANADIAN POLICYMAKERS

In this section, I briefly discuss three demographic considerations which, I argue, receive too little attention in most standard analyses of the subject: first, the fact that an urban route to the future complements the more visible reserve-based self-government route; second, intermarriage; and third, the large number of individuals of Aboriginal ancestry who do not identify as Aboriginal. While these three foci would need extensive supplementation if a comprehensive examination of First Nation realities was to be undertaken, they merit special attention for several reasons. Most importantly, they typically receive much less attention than their importance appears to justify. With a few limited exceptions, it is not unreasonable to speak of a culture of avoidance surrounding these subjects. The near taboo status of these subjects stems from the perception that their discussion is an unwelcome intrusion or distraction from the manner in which the dominant paradigm defines the situation. To draw attention to these three realities, therefore, simultaneously directs attention to the highly politicized nature of the policy debate about First Nations futures.

Two Roads to the Future

Neither the general Aboriginal nor the more specific First Nations reality is confined to land-based communities. For First Nations there are two routes to the future. First, there is the reserve-based landed community with boundaries, a resident population with a history of living together since the establishment of the reserve, a legal status under the *Indian Act*, and governing authorities. This, the overwhelming focus of political and scholarly attention, is supplemented by a diaspora population of over 40 percent of the total legal status population living off-reserve and distributed in large metropolitan centres, in smaller urban centres, in frontier communities, and in various community and local circumstances in-between.

The off-reserve population, which (partly due to Bill C-31 reinstatements) increased from 30 percent of the status Indian population in 1981 to 43 percent in 2001 (Canada. DIAND 2002, xvi, xii), is under-studied. It is heterogeneous, coming from many different First Nations, supplemented by a large Métis element, especially in western Canada, and a non-status component. The non-status component of the First Nation urban population will grow rapidly, fed by the contribution of high intermarriage rates in urban settings and the loss of legal status for the children of two successive out-marriages in the grandparent and parent generation.

Urban natives have a more fluid population than reserve-based communities. They also lack the obvious focus provided by a land base and an identifiable political leadership. Nevertheless, Andersen convincingly argues that "Aboriginal people" (Métis, Cree, Dene, Anishnabe, etc.) have created "urban *Native* communities ... new and distinct communities ... [and] new cultural norms" (Andersen 2002, 19-20). He goes on to make the "larger point ... that urban Native communities represent *new* forms of *Native* culture" (ibid., 24).[20]

Both paths to the future require research and policy attention.[21] The non-territorial, largely urban route lacks the clear focus provided by nationalism and the greater potential for self-government of territorially based First Nations, or of Nunavut. It nevertheless deserves no less attention for the simple reason, if no other, that more than half of the indigenous population, or slightly less, depending on the criteria employed, is travelling on it.

The non-territorial, largely urban route merits attention for the additional reason that it is home to contradictory developments. City life for urban Aboriginals is in a "high state of flux," with "family instability" and "residential instability" leading to "turbulence in urban communities" (Norris and Clatworthy 2003, 69 and 73). Incontrovertible evidence confirms the emergence of an urban underclass characterized by urban gangs (Humphreys 1999), crime, drug abuse, prostitution and for many a ghetto existence.[22] LaPrairie notes how "normalized and 'everyday' violence had become a constant for many people" (LaPrairie 1995, 433; see also 85, 387). According to another study, even a "casual visitor" would see "all the ... signals that mark the emergence of Canada's first US style slum" in Winnipeg, as well as in "Regina and to some extent in other Prairie cities" (Mendelson and Battle 1999, 25). These are the factors that encouraged RCAP to contrast "healthy, sustainable [First Nation] communities that create the conditions for a rounded life [with] ... an essentially alien urban environment [leading to] ... a rootless urban existence" (Canada 1996, vol. 2(2), 1023).

However, in marked contrast to this negative portrayal, other data is much more positive about the off-reserve, largely urban population, pointing to higher incomes, lower unemployment, superior educational attainment, the highest life expectancy among Aboriginal peoples, and a lesser incidence of social breakdown than in the on-reserve Indian population in terms of family violence, rape, alcohol, and drug abuse and suicide (Cairns 2000*a*, ch. 4; see also Beavon and Cooke 1998; Simpson 1998; and Cairns 2000*c*). As Newhouse and Peters suggest, RCAP not only marginalized urban Aboriginal peoples in its report, but viewed them through the distorting "lens of deficiency and [cultural] erosion" (Newhouse and Peters 2003*b*, 8; and Newhouse 2003, 251). Additional evidence is provided by Beavon and Cooke who, in a direct comparison of Registered Indians on and off reserve, found that the latter "fared substantially better" than on-reserve Indians in terms of the United Nations Human Development Index, measuring gross domestic product (GDP) per capita, educational attainment, and life expectancy at birth. This was true in all regions of the country (Beavon and Cooke 2003, 209, 217 and 219).[23]

Some of the relatively positive off-reserve data reflects what Guimond calls "ethnic mobility," or "ethnic drift," which refers to individuals changing their self-identification from non-Aboriginal to Aboriginal. According to Guimond, this ethnic mobility "is taking place outside Indian reserves, mostly in urban centres" (Guimond 2003, 100). Since these ethnic "drifters" have higher educational attainments than the stable Aboriginal identifiers the more positive educational statistics in part reflect identity mobility. Presumably, some of the other positive statements in the preceding paragraph are also products of ethnic mobility.[24]

The contradictory aspects of the Aboriginal urban reality described above and the limited research devoted to the urban scene argue for a much greater policy and research focus on urban Aboriginal life.

The disproportionate contemporary policy focus on reserve communities is over-determined by history, by the complications of federalism, by the federal government policy focus on reserve communities, by the diffuse nature of the urban Aboriginal presence, and by the fact that the heady language of nation more easily applies to reserve communities with their own government, and by other factors. (Cairns 2000c). This policy and research bias is, however, under-justified in terms of democratic criteria (the off-reserve numbers involved), in terms of the ill-understood contrast between ghetto realities and an emerging Aboriginal middle class,[25] and in terms of the stark reality that there clearly are two routes to the future.[26] "City life," as Newhouse and Peters report, "is now an integral component of Aboriginal peoples' lives in Canada" (Newhouse and Peters 2003b, 5).

Intermarriage

It is neither possible nor desirable to assess the future of and policy for the First Nations population without acknowledging the extent of intermarriage. Intermarriage rates, defined as marriage or cohabitation between a person with legal Indian status and one without that status, are very high; although the non-status person may, of course, be Aboriginal. Off-reserve figures for the five-year period ending 31 December 1995 hover slightly below 58 percent, while the on-reserve figure is somewhat less than 23 percent (Four Directions Consulting Group 1997, 20). When two out-marriages in a row result in a loss of legal status for the children, out-marriage rates threaten the long-run survival of the legal status population. By mid-century, the legal status population will begin to decline. A number of small bands near urban centres will legally disappear in coming decades. "In the long term," according to Clatworthy,

Bill C-31's rules concerning Indian registration "will lead to the extinction of First Nations (as defined under the *Indian Act*)" (Clatworthy 2003, 88).

Intermarriage verges on taboo status as an object of academic attention. The Royal Commission paid scant attention to it, and the academic community, with few exceptions, leaves it alone.[27] When I tried to draw attention to the obvious significance of intermarriage at a small seminar with RCAP commissioners, the mood quickly became uncomfortable and I was discouraged by the Chair from proceeding. This relative silence is extraordinary, given the fact that minority communities concerned for their own cultural survival typically view intermarriage with apprehension, and thus accord the subject high priority as a research area.

To treat intermarriage as a taboo subject is to privilege ignorance of a key vehicle for the transmission of values and identities between members of First Nations and other Canadians, and to reduce our understanding of a reality that contributes to different life styles between on-reserve and off-reserve populations.

Ancestry Population

Census data employed by RCAP divides the Aboriginal population into those with Aboriginal ancestry and those with Aboriginal identity. Overall, about one-third of the ancestry population does not declare an Aboriginal identity. There are, however, immense variations between the percentage of the ancestry population that carries an Aboriginal identity. In Montreal and Halifax only 22 percent and 32 percent respectively of the Aboriginal ancestry population reported an Aboriginal identity. In Regina, 94 percent of the Aboriginal ancestry population reports an Aboriginal identity, and 92 percent do so in Saskatoon (see Siggner 2003*b*, 16; and see Cairns 2000*a*, 126-28 for a discussion based on earlier figures).

Our relative ignorance of the ancestry-non-identity population represents a huge gap in our understanding. Astonishingly, RCAP restricts its observation on this subject to a cryptic footnote reporting "some evidence that [they have] socio-economic characteristics quite similar to those of Canadians as a whole, while those who do identify as Aboriginals have quite different socio-economic characteristics" (Canada 1996, vol. 1, 24 n.7). If the commission's speculations based on "some evidence" are correct, the overall urban Aboriginal ancestry population would present a much more positive image of urban life than the smaller population of those who self-identify as Aboriginal.

Andy Siggner, Senior Advisor on Aboriginal Statistics, Statistics Canada, recently compiled data on education, employment, and income for the Aboriginal origins/no Aboriginal identity category and for the Aboriginal identity population. Thirteen percent of the former had university degrees, compared to 4 percent of the identity population; moreover, 63 percent of the former and 44 percent of the latter were employed. Average total income for the former was $22,000, $6,000 more than for the Aboriginal Identity population (1996 figures). Unfortunately, the figures do not specify the location of this population as urban or otherwise (Siggner 2002).[28]

The most plausible reason for the commission's otherwise inexplicable unwillingness to analyze and report on the non-identifying Aboriginal ancestry population — a reason mentioned by various informants — is that this very large group could be portrayed as an example of successful assimilation, and thus employed as counter-evidence to the dominant and preferred nationalist discourse. Be that as it may, the lack of knowledge about and near systematic avoidance of the non-identifying Aboriginal ancestry category by the research community profoundly distorts our understanding of the Aboriginal reality that policymakers seek to influence. We would be much better informed about the identifying Aboriginal population if we had more studies of the Aboriginal ancestry population that does not identify as Aboriginal. Our knowledge of each would be greatly enhanced by knowledge of the other.

These three characteristics of First Nation and Aboriginal life, each in its own way, qualify portrayals that implicitly or explicitly define the First Nations reality in terms of homogeneous communities with little connection to, or cultural sharing with, their non-Aboriginal neighbours. The large off-reserve component of First Nations, supplemented by Métis and non-status Indians, means that policy and attention which overwhelmingly focus on reserve communities, typically now described as "nations," undervalue the lives, needs, achievements, and experiences of 40 to 60 percent of the Aboriginal population (depending on the identification criteria employed). High rates of intermarriage suggest that portrayals of First Nations and the non-Aboriginal populations travelling on separate paths to separate destinations overlook and pay inadequate attention to the reality of interdependence in the most intimate areas of life. Finally, the gap between ancestry and identity figures (30 percent on the whole), and the immense variations in the size of the gap across the country, adds an overlooked complexity that has attracted negligible scholarly attention. Any policy discussion that pays scant attention to the human realities behind this data deprives policymakers of essential information.

The probable explanation for the limited attention-getting capacity of the urban situation, of intermarriage, and of the large Aboriginal ancestry group that does not proclaim Aboriginal identity is that they do not easily fit into the dominant discourse that stresses self-government, cultural difference, nationhood, and a distinct Aboriginal route to the future. On the contrary, they suggest extensive inter-cultural contact, especially in urban settings, intercultural intimacy in marriage and cohabitation, and divergent futures for reserve-based communities and off-reserve, mainly urban populations.[29] These observations, however, need to be qualified by recognizing the extensive movement in both directions between reserve and city for First Nation members with status (Norris and Beavon 1999).

SMALL POPULATIONS AND OTHER PRACTICAL CONCERNS

The importance of population size for the quality and jurisdictional capacity of self-government also merits an extensive attention it has not received.[30]

The politics of nationalism gets in the way of the accurate presentation and evaluation of data capable of influencing the plausibility of various futures. This is evident in public discourse and academic literature that pays limited and inadequate attention to the small population of individual First Nations. RCAP should be partly exempted from this critique.[31] It was deeply concerned about the small size of Indian bands. It recognized that federal policy-making that chose bands rather than nations or tribal organizations as the basic political-administrative unit, "[broke] up ... Aboriginal and treaty nations into smaller and smaller units ... as a deliberate step toward assimilation of Aboriginal individuals into the larger society" (Canada 1996, vol. 2, 89). RCAP accordingly proposed a comprehensive process to encourage consolidation. "The Commission," it asserted, "considers the right of self-determination to be vested in Aboriginal nations rather than small local communities" (ibid., 166).

The viability of a response to First Nations nationalism will be increased if policymakers keep in mind various realities which, cumulatively, suggest that First Nations should be located in the category of "micro-nations."[32] By way of illustration, only 5.6 percent of Indian bands, 35 out of 627, have on-reserve populations of more than 2,000; nearly two-thirds of Indian bands have on-reserve populations of less than 500. One hundred and four bands have on-reserve populations of less than one hundred (Canada. DIAND 2002, xv).[33] These figures were deeply troubling to RCAP. Many of the over 600 Indian bands had "nation" in their official titles — a descriptive label most frequently added in the last two decades. The umbrella political organization that acts and speaks on their behalf is the Assembly of First Nations. The Royal Commission rejected "nation" as an appropriate label for very small communities on the premise that small populations lacked the capacity to assume the governing responsibilities it proposed, and also could not effectively play the nation role in the "nation-to-nation" relationship that RCAP asserted was to be the primary relationship between Aboriginal peoples and the Canadian state. RCAP then proposed a consolidation of the existing 600 plus bands, supplemented by Inuit and Métis communities, into 60–80 nations by way of aggregation and various forms of merger.[34]

There is a fundamental ambiguity at the heart of the RCAP report, a report of over 3,500 pages based on the most extensive round of hearings and the most massive research program on Aboriginal policy undertaken in Canadian history. On the one hand, nation is to be the basic political unit for Aboriginal peoples, and nation-to-nation is to be the fundamental relationship with Canada. These are the crucial structuring concepts for the report. On the other hand, its numerical criteria for nationhood (an average population of 5–7,000), in order to enhance governing capacity and community viability, excludes the bulk of Indian peoples as presently constituted from nation status and hence from its ideal nation-to-nation relationship. Following the RCAP analysis, in the vast majority of cases, nations will have to be created (or perhaps re-created on the basis of historic nations) by reducing the number of distinct, separate Indian communities/bands by about 90 percent.

In general, therefore, nation is a project for the future. In a sense, the Royal Commission gambled. It has more to say about the nations it hopes will emerge given appropriate incentives than it does about the reality that now exists of hundreds of bands too small to meet the commission's criteria for nationhood. If those small bands remain the reality on the ground, the commission goal of a multinational Canada and nation-to-nation relations is unattainable, for very few First Nation members will live in nations. The aggregation of existing bands into nations is an extraordinarily ambitious goal, the achievement of which would require a herculean process of nation-building. The federal government is lukewarm to such a proposal, in part because it has to deal with existing Indian bands embedded in the *Indian Act*. Further, any consolidation proposal challenges the existing leadership in over 600 First Nation communities. Not surprisingly, the Assembly of First Nations offers little support for a proposal that undercuts the base of its political constituency. Further, in some cases, the cost of consolidation may be political instability before the new arrangement jells. Finally, even a successful consolidation still leaves policymakers and the governments of these emergent entities with populations that are relatively small (5–7,000 on average, as already noted).

If the existing population size of legally defined Indian bands remains largely unaltered, except by birth, death, mobility, and intermarriage; if the land mass of most reserves remains of "minuscule size" (Morse 2002*b*, 10);[35] if there is little or no population consolidation into larger entities, "vibrant economies" will be exceptions, although generous land-claim settlements will benefit a few communities (ibid., 11). This outcome is reinforced by the fact that nearly 45 percent of Indian reserves are rural, 3.7 percent are remote, and nearly 17 percent are without year-round road access to a service centre (2001 data) (Canada. DIAND 2003, 16).[36] In these circumstances, the jurisdictional capacity that can be assumed by the majority of First Nation governments is severely limited, and so, accordingly, is their capacity to either preserve or modernize their indigenous cultures.[37]

Kymlicka's observations are relevant to this discussion. He asserts that "to maintain [what he calls] a separate societal culture in a modern state is an immensely ambitious and arduous project" (Kymlicka 1998, 31). It requires "the use of, and control over, a variety of political powers and institutions" (ibid., 34). In *Multicultural Citizenship*, he argues that such a culture "provides its members with meaningful ways of life across the full range of human activities, including social, educational, religious, recreational, and economic life, encompassing both public and private spheres." Such a culture has to be "institutionally embodied — in schools, media, economy, government, etc." (Kymlicka 1995, 76). Tellingly, he observes that the province of Quebec, with jurisdiction and population beyond the dreams of Aboriginal leaders, continues to feel culturally and linguistically threatened. After listing some of the jurisdictions and policies employed by Quebec, he asserts that "similar conditions are required for sustaining indigenous societies in Canada and around the world" (Kymlicka 1998, 34). Such "similar conditions," unfortunately, are clearly absent and unattainable for the small populations previously noted.[38] Even larger First Nations — either those that now exist or that may emerge from consolidations — are only considered to be large because other First Nations are so small.

An important exception may be emerging in Saskatchewan where "a province-wide system of First Nations governments, representing over 115,000 members and over 70 communities [is under serious discussion]. The First Nations governance system would include a single province-wide government, a series of about five regional governments (based on tribal areas or treaty areas), and over 70 community First Nation governments" (Hawkes 2002, 7). Programs and services would be provided both on- and off-reserve in some circumstances. A key rationale for this encouraging development is "the need to aggregate First Nations jurisdiction in order to provide for meaningful self-government" (ibid., 9 and 12-13).

There is a clear need for social science research in two key problem areas. First, what incentives will encourage successful mergers and consolidations of small communities in order to create more viable populations for governing purposes? For example, if the Saskatchewan experiment succeeds, what can be done to duplicate it elsewhere? Second, we need research that creatively explores the possibilities, however limited, of cultural retention and invigoration for small communities.[39] Under optimal conditions, what can small communities locked in interdependence with the environing society achieve?[40]

Some degree of qualified optimism might be reasonable if a small community seeks to opt out of as much of modernity as possible. This, however, does not appear to be the First Nation or Aboriginal reality. According to RCAP, Aboriginal communities must participate "in global society," and "in a global economy," and should have the same living standards and "quality of life as other Canadians." In the future, Aboriginal people should be proportionally represented in all the prestigious professions from "doctors [to] ... computer specialists ... [to] archaeologists and other careers" (Cairns 2000a, 123). This is not the language of opt-out, or of dismissing the norms and practices of non-Aboriginal society. Neither, however, is it the language of assimilation.

We are operating in uncharted territory where the past offers little guidance. The content of the inherent right of self-government and the manner of its implementation are "by no means clear," according to Cameron and Wherrett, "and its specification requires complex negotiations in which the parameters of the exercise are necessarily obscure to both sides" (Cameron and Wherrett 1995, 91). Kerry Wilkins, a passionate supporter of self-government, nevertheless agrees that numerous problems, which receive scant attention in the literature, need to be addressed. He is both surprised and perturbed by the passionate advocacy in favour of judicial recognition of a constitutionally entrenched right of self-government at a time when we lack "a shared and trustworthy understanding, even in outline, of how self-government rights would work within mainstream legal arrangements or of the impact they may have on them" (Wilkins 2000, 247, 244-45 and 249). He goes on to raise, always in a supportive voice, the concern that some communities lack the varied leadership skills, and technical training appropriate to the needs of their members. He expresses concern about vulnerable individuals, especially women, in communities where accountability is weakened by the fact that most government revenues come from outside the community (ibid., 254 and 258). His apprehension is shared by many members of Aboriginal communities who have lost "trust and confidence in community leadership and governance arrangements" (ibid., 268). He concludes by noting concerns about the capacity of the Canadian state to incorporate 600 plus small governments into Canadian institutions, including the intergovernmental structure of federalism (ibid., 200, 259 n. 58 and 260).

Wilkins' basic point is that in spite of the extensive academic attention to, political discussion of, and judicial observations concerning self-government some of the practicalities and normative concerns have been insufficiently addressed. Although he does not provide explanations for this failure of attention, clues are dropped here and there. Nationalism reacting to a colonized past discourages attention to impediments to self-determination. Advocates of the inherent right of self-government are almost inevitably hostile to the intrusion of practical concerns that outsiders might employ to weaken the exercise of the right. In addition, the leading role of the academic legal community and the level of abstraction of legal analysis discourage attention to practical concerns. Moreover, there is a certain reluctance among supporters of First Nations to identify difficulties and impediments to the successful exercise of the right of self-government. This reluctance is reinforced by suggestions in the vein of American Indian activist, Vine Deloria Jr., that the time has come when *We Talk, You Listen* (Deloria 1970). Although Wilkins does not refrain from speaking, he is clearly somewhat hesitant about his role, obviously concerned that his admonition to slow down and sort out certain problems in advance may be misunderstood as putting him in the wrong camp.[41] He would no doubt agree with Noel Dyck, who some years ago wrote an article on the difficulties of "Telling it like it is," when to do so might get in the way of the self-government which he, and most other anthropologists, supported (Dyck 1995).

It is truly remarkable how the small size of First Nation communities and other practical concerns receive such limited attention. The BC Treaty Commission, in "A Review of the Treaty Process," included with the *Annual*

Report for 2001, recently asserted that it was unclear how "the inherent right of Aboriginal peoples to govern themselves" could be meaningfully exercised by First Nations with very small populations, or who lacked experience of "strong governance." The review observed that the federal and provincial governments had squarely addressed the issue, nor had First Nations (BC Treaty Commission 2002*a*, 7 and 10). The time has come for such issues to gain the attention they deserve.

A desirable goal, implementing the inherent right of self-government, gets mired in complexity as we look beyond the right to various seemingly inescapable realities. Some of the language we use does a disservice to the cause it is intended to serve. Small nations with limited capacities, and with colonized histories that have too often generated malaise and deep dysfunction have to find some accommodation with the existing society and its institutional/constitutional arrangements. Many of the relevant questions, as Wilkins observes, have scarcely been asked, let alone answered.

First Nations are micro-nations. We need to keep in mind the adjective as well as the noun. Micro-nations cannot by themselves handle macro-tasks. They can, however, if proper conditions exist, handle functions appropriate to their capacity. The Harvard Project on American Indian Economic Development has demonstrated that self-government, if modelled on appropriate criteria, can be highly effective. These criteria, which Joseph Kalt and his colleagues have communicated to Canadian audiences, are the following:

- *Practical sovereignty*, giving real control of relevant issues and effective decision-making powers to Indian nations;
- *Capable governing institutions*, including an autonomous court system; and
- *Cultural match*, meaning the institutions of government and First Nations culture should match.

To these are added two supplementary considerations:

- *Leadership:* individuals with the vision and capacity to break away from the status quo and who can see a path to a better future; and
- *Strategic orientation:* leaving the management of crises behind and thinking and acting in terms of the long run.

These criteria do not guarantee success, but they do increase the possibility of attaining it more frequently. They are criteria that seek to mobilize local leadership in tune with local culture and local economic and other realities (Cornell, Jorgensen and Kalt 2002; BC Treaty Commission 2002*b*; Cornell 2000; Cornell and Kalt 1992).

The achievement of self-government will probably fall short of the goals of its most passionate supporters. It remains, nevertheless, a desirable goal. The attainment of self-government, however, does not mean that the relation of federal and provincial governments to self-governing First Nations and their people suddenly becomes irrelevant. The small size of First Nations and the limitations on governing capacities that necessarily involves mean that many policies, regulations, and services will continue to come from federal and provincial governments. Self-government, no matter how ambitious and successful, is not enough. Virtually all the great affairs of state will continue to be handled by federal and provincial governments. Further, the needs and desires of the 60 percent of the Aboriginal population that is mainly urban, which is heterogeneous and lacks a land base, requires sympathetic policies from federal, provincial, and municipal governments. We need to think of the total constitutional order, not just the limited escape from its functioning offered by self-government for small populations.

Some of the difficulties of coming to grips with the complexities of a country-wide scheme of First Nations self-government relate to realities such as small size, isolation, and a weak economic base discussed above. Others are linked to a diffuse alienation from the overall Canadian constitutional order. The result is that a focused practical discussion of self-government is frustrated by an imperfectly joined larger debate relating to the goal toward which First Nations and other Canadians are headed.

ALIENATION FROM THE CANADIAN CONSTITUTIONAL ORDER

The premise behind the following discussion is that the constitutional task is to fit First Nations into a modified version of the existing constitutional order in which members of First Nations will be citizens of their nation and of Canada, and in which First Nation governments are constitutionally protected. First Nation peoples will, in other words, have a special status. It is possible to argue the contrary, that they should be extricated from the federal-provincial confederation and located in a second treaty confederation parallel to and outside the existing federal-provincial order. This is James Tully's proposal, still in its early stages.[42] Until the proposal is more fully fleshed out, it is difficult to judge whether its desirability is matched by its viability. At the moment I am doubtful; hence, in the following pages I view constitutional alienation as a problem to be overcome within a modified version of the existing constitutional order rather than viewing the latter as an imperialist legacy to be escaped from.

Yesterday: Assimilation of Individuals

Historically, the official goal of the Indian policy was assimilation. Indians were viewed as immigrants who had arrived early. The 1969 White Paper assumed the validity of the goal but argued that the ostensible means for its achievement — treaties, isolation on reserves, a special act singling Indians out from the general population, and an idiosyncratic place in the federal system — were in fact impediments.[43] The White Paper proposed dismantling the battery of differential policies and administration and transforming Indians into standard Canadians. Had the White Paper achieved its objectives, individual Indians would have had the same relation to the major institutions of the constitutional order as other Canadians. There would have been no problem of "fit," which was simply assumed. The existing constitutional framework would have welcomed Indians as individuals and members of communities in a supportive manner similar to how the international system of independent states welcomed the newly independent Third World nations casting off the shackles of empire.

From the perspective of governments and the non-Aboriginal population, assimilation had many advantages. It was psychologically gratifying with its reassuring message that admission to membership in the majority culture was an obvious good, the availability of which reflected the generosity and openness of the majority. It would end the anomalous status of a people whose lives were governed by special arrangements which distanced them from the normal constitutional order. By so doing, it left the latter unchanged. The constitutional order did not have to bend to accommodate Indianness. Rather, Indians were to travel along the assimilation path until they were ready for full membership in an unchanged constitutional order. The "gift" offered by the larger society was not respect for Indian difference, but rather undifferentiated inclusion.

Now: Survival as Nations

The contemporary discourse of Aboriginal rights is dramatically opposed to the assimilatory assumptions behind the White Paper and the historic policy of incorporating Indians into an unaltered set of constitutional and institutional arrangements — parliament, federalism, the inherited first-past-the-post electoral system, etc. Not only have "nations" displaced individuals as the entities that have to be accommodated, but that accommodation presupposes a significantly modified constitutional order, and indeed a new definition of Canada. Accordingly, the fit between the goal of Indian policy and the inherited constitutional/institutional order, which was assumed by the non-Aboriginal policymakers up to the defeat of the White Paper, no longer exists.[44] Although the data is fragmentary and somewhat fugitive, there appears to be widespread alienation, particularly of Indian peoples, from the constitutional order.

Alienation

It is not surprising that many members of First Nations accord limited legitimacy to the major institutions of the Canadian constitutional order. For most of the first century after Confederation (1867) their treatment is appropriately described as "constitutional stigmatization" (Cairns 1999*b*). "From birth to death," argued Noel Dyck, "most Indians have been caught in a situation where they have had to listen to one unvarying and unceasing message — that they are unacceptable as they are and that to become worthwhile as individuals they must change in the particular manner advocated by their current tutelage agents" (Dyck 1991, 27).[45] Indian policy was an education in not belonging. Taylor reminds us that this imperial practice and supporting belief system is a form of abusive misrecognition that can inflict "a grievous wound" on its recipients (Taylor 1992, 26). The Middle-East scholar, Albert Hourani, put it even more strongly: "To be in someone else's power is a conscious experience which induces doubts about the ordering of the universe" (Irwin 2001, 30). To be colonized is experienced as a disruption, as a change of cultural direction imposed rather than chosen. It naturally translates into an ambivalence about the culture of the imperial master, an ambivalence frequently manifested in anger, rage, and confusion of identity.

Patricia Monture-Angus, a Mohawk scholar, recently responded to this heritage of humiliation with the assertion that "as part of my personal commitment to 'unlearn' colonization I refuse to think of this land as Canada, Ontario, Quebec, and so on. When I travel I think in terms of whose territory I am visiting — the Cree, the Algonquin, the Dene and so on" (1995, 245 n. 13). Brad Morse, a leading non-Aboriginal legal scholar, agrees with Monture-Angus' negative assessment of "the history of colonization ... an unmitigated disaster from the perspective of Aboriginal peoples and from the view of any neutral observer" (Morse 2002*a*, 92-93). This history has produced widespread First Nations "mistrust and suspicion" of federal proposals for change (Morse 2002*b*, 37 and 2). Indeed, mistrust and suspicion are recurrently identified in encounters between First Nations and the political authorities of the Canadian state.[46] This manifests itself in matters large and small. A sizeable number of First Nations refuse to allow their communities to be included in the census (Goldmann and Siggner 1995, 265).[47] For example, the 1996 data reported an Aboriginal population of 72,000 in Quebec, 9,000 less than the previous census in 1986, a result partly explained by the non-participation of communities with a combined population of 15,500 (Morse 2002*a*, 80).

Parliament and Voters

Widespread suspicion and wariness translate into a limited identification with the major institutions of the Canadian state. Parliament is not seen as a sympathetic arena generating positive outcomes. RCAP speaks of the "inherent ineffectiveness of the democratic political relationship as seen by Aboriginal peoples ... such representation, when cast in terms of conventional democracy, is itself regarded as illegitimate. Aboriginal peoples seek nation-to-nation political relations, and these cannot be achieved simply by representation in

Canadian political institutions" (Canada 1996, vol.1, 249).[48] Georges Erasmus, before becoming co-chair of RCAP, spoke scathingly of the incapacity of Parliament to represent First Nation concerns. The "bland assertion," he argued, "that First Nations and their governments are represented by non-aboriginal politicians who have no interest, demonstrated or latent, in advocating our rights is bogus and without foundation in fact or action" (Canada 1987, 2201). Given this dismissive attitude to parliamentary representation, the antipathy of RCAP, co-chaired by Erasmus, to legislatures was to be expected.[49]

Ovide Mercredi, who succeeded Erasmus as National Chief, giving evidence in 1990 to the Royal Commission on Electoral Reform and Party Financing, agreed with his predecessor: "What good is your democracy, when you can use your majority, as you have in the past and will surely do in the future, to suppress our collective indigenous rights and freedoms? ... For us the one person one vote foundation for electoral power only translates into white majority rule, and, in the absence of any political power we are the objects of governmental decisions and actions that deprive us of the benefits of democratic governments" (Mercredi 1990, 3).[50]

The limited legitimacy of Parliament is shown in many ways. Voting turnout is well below the Canadian average. According to Malloy and White, who underline the tension and distrust in Aboriginal-Canadian government relations, "natives do not place a high priority on voting in Canadian elections." According to many, voting for candidates and membership in legislatures "gives unwarranted legitimacy to non-native governments" (Malloy and White 1997, 60, 62).[51] Some bands even refuse to allow polling booths on their reserves.[52]

An examination of Aboriginal voting participation in the Maritime provinces found a striking decline in New Brunswick and Nova Scotia from the 1960s to the 1990s, which contrasted with very high participation in band elections. The authors interpreted the decline as due to a "change in consciousness — from Canadians who are Indians, to members of the Maliseet or Micmac nations ... [explained as] a rejection of the Canadian electoral process as an alien one, a political process of a state which is not their own ... one could argue that their 'sense of civic duty' as Canadians has all but disappeared as they see themselves less and less as Canadians" (Bedford and Pobihuschy 1994, 29).[53]

The preceding observations in this section, while no doubt true at a general level, encounter significant exceptions in the territorial politics of northern Canada, and perhaps elsewhere. The election of the first Legislative Assembly of Nunavut in 1999 had a turnout of 88.59 percent (Chief Electoral Officer, Nunavut, 1999, 28).[54] The 1999 election to the Legislative Assembly of the Northwest Territories recorded a voting turnout of 70.5 percent (Chief Electoral Officer, Northwest Territories, 2000, 1).[55] In the Yukon, the percentage of electors who voted was 79.58 percent in 1996, 78.58 percent in 2000, and 78.13 percent in 2002 (Chief Electoral Officer, Yukon, 2000, for 1996 and 2000 figures, and Chief Electoral Officer, Yukon 2003 for the 2002 election).[56] In all three northern territories, the constituency electorates are small and personal knowledge of the candidate is higher than in southern Canada. In addition, both the indigenous percentage of the electorate and the number of indigenous candidates are very high, especially in Nunavut and the Northwest Territories, compared to southern Canada.[57] Further, the significance of government in the economy, when the private sector is weak, provides additional incentives to vote.

Confusion of Voice

The limited legitimacy of Parliament is implicit in the role of the Assembly of First Nations (AFN) as a recognized spokesperson for First Nation concerns. This was indicated by its participation, along with other major Aboriginal organizations, in the four special constitutional conferences (1983 to 1987) to clarify the Aboriginal and treaty rights identified in section 35 of the *Constitution Act, 1982,* and again in the discussions that produced the Charlottetown Accord. These recognitions not only suggest that the AFN is not a simple interest group, but that it has an informally recognized, albeit shaky, constitutional status. The logical corollary is that even though members of First Nations possess the federal franchise, Parliament has a diminished capacity to speak on behalf of First Nations and their members. The inevitable result is a profound tension between the AFN and the federal government (particularly INAC), a tension that cannot always be kept under control. It surfaced strikingly in the polemical exchanges over the First Nations Governance proposal, in which AFN National Chief Matthew Coon Come and INAC Minister Robert Nault denied credibility to the other.[58] (The act was subsequently withdrawn by the federal government when Paul Martin replaced Jean Chrétien as prime minister in 2003.)

The dispute over the governance proposal highlighted competing constitutional theories. The federal government insisted on its right to speak directly to Aboriginal peoples as Canadian citizens, thus bypassing the chiefs. The AFN criticized this direct consultation for undercutting First Nations leadership and insisted on nation-to-nation negotiations (Chase 2001; Flanagan 2001). The subsequent withdrawal of the *Governance Act* was the latest example of a stalemate born of the conflict of competing legitimacies — the legitimacy that flows from First Nations nationalism and the legitimacy that attaches to the authority of the sovereign state.

Constitutional Ambivalence

This tension has structural roots in that Parliament and the AFN have rival claims, both based on the constitution, to represent and speak for First Nations communities and their members. Indian and Northern Affairs Canada is responsible for the *Indian Act,* an expression of federal legislative authority based on section 91(24) of the original *BNA Act, 1867*, dealing with "Indians and Lands Reserved for the Indians." The AFN and other national Aboriginal organizations identify with the recently constitutionalized section 35 (1) and (2) of the *Constitution Act, 1982* which recognizes and affirms "the existing Aboriginal and treaty rights of the Aboriginal peoples of Canada," defined as including the "Indian, Inuit and Métis peoples of Canada." Section 91(24) reflects a colonial past now held in disrepute when Indians were wards, and Indian policy was made as a matter of course by non-indigenous legislators representing non-indigenous voters. Sections 35 (1) and (2) are constitutionalized expressions of anti-colonialism. Section 35 is a positive affirmation of Aboriginal difference supported by and embedded in Aboriginal and treaty rights.[59] Section 35 is the focal point for contemporary Aboriginal jurisprudence. Prior to 1982 the Crown could unilaterally extinguish Aboriginal and treaty rights. While it may be an exaggeration to label the coexistence of 91(24) and 35 (1) and (2) as creating a constitutionally stimulated deadlock, it is surely reasonable to identify their coexistence as reflecting a serious degree of constitutional incoherence — the meeting ground of a past vision and a future vision.[60]

The suspicious, often hostile attitudes of First Nations, of chiefs and councils, and of the AFN to the federal government are close to an inevitable response to the ambiguous face of Ottawa. On the one hand, the federal government is the site of a legislature (and the Cabinet and prime minister it supports) based on universal suffrage (including members of First Nations). It is also, however, home to an Indian affairs bureaucracy, with its own Cabinet minister, administering an *Indian Act* universally disparaged as a colonial legacy with a long expired shelf-life that survives only because of disagreement over how to get rid of it.[61] The surviving colonial reality gets in the way of a First Nation allegiance to, identification with, and electoral participation in a political system that has been unable to shed the administrative and statutory legacies of a colonial past.

The rivalry between two patterns of representation triggered by a constitution caught in the transition between past and future was played out in the Royal Commission on Aboriginal Peoples. As already noted, not only was there an Aboriginal majority of commissioners, but the co-chair had been National Chief of the AFN, and two other commissioners had held influential positions in Aboriginal organizations. Presumably, they were selected because of their past representative role in Aboriginal organizations, whose very existence presupposed the inadequacy of Parliament to represent Aboriginal interests. RCAP's proposal for a new third chamber to represent Aboriginal nations, coupled with a dismissive attitude toward elections and the House of Commons, elaborated the rationale, which for a quarter of a century had somewhat inchoately justified a special place for Aboriginal peoples and their political organizations in Canadian public life. The RCAP proposal was designed to enhance identification with indigenous nations over identification as a Canadian citizen. In addition, the report's recommendations included numerous ongoing important roles for the major Aboriginal organizations (Canada 1996, vol. 5). These were steps toward the commission's goal of a multinational Canada in which the actors were nations and wherein citizens were to be defined in relation to the nations to which they belonged.

Disaffection from Federal and Provincial Governments

Disenchantment with the federal government does not translate into affection for the provinces. Historically, First Nation members had an anomalous relationship to the federal system. Prior to the post-World War II extension of the federal and provincial franchise to Indians, they experienced a virtual unitary state relationship with the federal government. They were not thought of and did not think of themselves as belonging to provincial communities, or as having the standard citizen relationship with provincial governments. The combination of a special statute, the *Indian Act*, a federal Indian Affairs Branch to administer it, and isolation on federally established and federally administered reserves inevitably meant that both practically and psychologically Indians existed outside the federal system. In 1966, the Hawthorn report noted that: "Historically the Canadian Indian has had an especially strong link with the federal government and a weak and tenuous relationship with provincial governments.... The Indians ... developed a special emotional bond with the federal government and suspicious and hostile attitudes to the provincial governments" (Hawthorn 1966/67, part I, 199). More recent research studies of individual provinces undertaken for RCAP, supplemented by other research, confirm the survival of negative attitudes to the provinces — ranging from hostile to wary and suspicious.[62] The "strong link with the federal government" noted by Hawthorn is prized as an indicator of the unique status of Indians, not because of a positive identification with Ottawa as such.

Uncertain Citizens

Given their anomalous position in the federal system, their historical experience as "outsiders" reflected in the denial of the federal franchise until 1960, and the fact that the traditional enfranchisement process required the relinquishment of Indian legal status in order to obtain the federal right to vote and to have the same relation to the federal government as other Canadians, it is not surprising that the label "uncertain citizens," in John Borrows' phrase, appropriately describes the widespread ambivalent contemporary relationship of Indian peoples to Canadian citizenship (Borrows 2001).[63] Borrows' assessment is supported with nuanced differences of tone by other scholars: Darlene Johnston, another First Nations author, refers to the "ambivalence and resistance that First Nations display toward Canadian citizenship" (Johnston 1993, 349).[64] Few Indians, she noted, chose the option of enfranchisement, the unhelpful label for giving up Indian status.[65]

The allegiance of members of First Nations to a state that was the agent of their victimization is, accordingly, problematic. Their psychological identification with the majority society is weakened by a nationalism conditioned by past experience which portrays that society negatively. For many, a citizenship connection to Canada becomes little more than a "regrettable necessity," instrumentally justified by the limited governing capacities of small populations and their needs for extensive fiscal infusions from outside (Carens 2000, 173). Similarly, Joyce Green notes a lack of agreement "among Aboriginal political and intellectual elites about the relevance and applicability of Canadian citizenship to Aboriginal peoples" (Green 2002, 7).

Explicit denials of Canadian citizenship emerge in the writings of several Aboriginal scholars (Alfred 1999, 19; Monture-Angus 1995, 167 n. 16; Monture-Angus 1999, 152 n. 1). Three of the six candidates for National Chief at the 1997 Assembly of First Nations leadership convention denied that they were Canadian (Bruyneel 2002*b*, 21-22), as does Matthew Coon Come, former National Chief (2000–2003) (Augustine and Richard 2002, 30). Taiaiake Alfred, while accepting that "a lot of our native people imagine themselves to be Canadians," asserts that they are victims of false consciousness, and "are 'in the darkness,' they have had their eyes shut to their true being, they can't envision a future in which we are nations" (Alfred 1999, xxi; see also 4).

Given the centrality of citizenship as the crucial symbol of political belonging, as the moral bond linking individuals to the state and to each other, the telling phrase "Uncertain citizens" underscores the distance that needs to be travelled before a harmonious co-habitation arrangement is reached.

Mixed Responses to the Charter

Ambivalent, sometimes hostile, attitudes to Canadian citizenship spill over into ambivalent attitudes to the application of the Charter to First Nation governments.[66] John Borrows, who supported the availability of the Charter to citizens of First Nation governments, described the debate about the Charter, a potent symbol of Canadianism, as extraordinarily divisive within First Nation communities (Borrows 1994, 21 and 31).

Borrows, observing the passionate support of the Native Women's Association of Canada for the application of the Charter to First Nation governments, was struck by the "tremendous lack of confidence that some First Nations women had in Aboriginal governments" (ibid., 45). Although he recognized the disruptive impact of the Charter, he did not see First Nation and Charter values as incongruous. Indeed, the arrival of the Charter could be an occasion for First Nations "to recapture the strength of principles which were often eroded through government interference" (ibid., 21).

Other assessments are less favourable. In 1989–90, in a frequently cited article, Mary Ellen Turpel, then a law professor and now a judge in Saskatchewan, authored a devastating root and branch critique of the Charter as wholly incompatible with Aboriginal values and beliefs (Turpel 1989/90). The "Charter's severest critics," according to Boldt and Long, "have been native Indians" (Boldt and Long 1985, 165). To be a Charter supporter was to be labelled a "dupe of the colonizing society" (Green 1993, 118). Although the Native Women's Association of Canada has been a strong supporter of its application to First Nation governments (Native Women's Association of Canada, n.d.), the Assembly of First Nations described it as a "foreign" document and passionately opposed its applicability and suitability for First Nation communities (First Nations Circle on the Constitution 1992, 64).[67]

There is well-argued support in main stream legal scholarship that as a matter of constitutional requirements the Charter does not apply to Aboriginal "communities exercising inherent self-government rights or powers" (Wilkins 1999, 62). If, however, the Charter does apply, the "acceptance of the [its] legitimacy would threaten the integrity of, and undermine internal respect for, the customs, traditions and orientations that constitute many indigenous forms of government" (ibid., 117).[68]

Boldt and Long agree with Turpel and the AFN on the cultural dissonance between the Charter and tribal traditions and beliefs. They go on, however, to note that in their contrast between the "western-liberal tradition and native American tribal philosophies," including "traditional customs relating to group rights," they are not arguing "that Indians are currently uniformly and consistently practising these traditions." In fact, these traditions have been "embraced as their charter myth" (Boldt and Long 1985, 169). In part, the appeal to tradition as a charter myth is a rhetorical weapon in the never-ending struggle to justify differentiated treatment. It is also a way to preserve identity integrity in the face of the ubiquitous pressures of the majority society.

In somewhat different language, opposition to the Charter comes from an appreciation of and antipathy to its (Canadian) nation-building goals. The Charter's nation-building purpose of linking Aboriginal peoples (and, of course, other Canadians as well) to the pan-Canadian state by the vehicle of rights confronts the rival nationalism of First Nations intent on preserving social and cultural difference from the pan-Canadian majority.

In addition, and quite apart from arguments about cultural differences and unhappiness with the fact that the nation-building purpose of the Charter is directed to the Canadian nation, the AFN opposition is based on the opposition of First Nation governments to constraints on their activities. The AFN vantage point is not that of scattered minorities seeking protection from majorities they distrust, but of First Nation governments who correctly see the Charter as a constraint. This component of Charter opposition, therefore, is similar to the opposition of the gang of eight provincial governments to the federal government backed Charter in the period leading up to the *Constitution Act, 1982*. In both cases, the opposition is to encroachments on the discretion of governments. For the provincial governments, opposition was expressed in the historic rhetoric of parliamentary supremacy. For First Nation elites, opposition was typically expressed in terms of the link between cultural difference and nationalism. The Charter was not their charter. Significantly, and supportive of the idea that Charter opposition is designed to protect First Nation governments from the constraint of rights, there does not appear to be any opposition to the Charter's availability for First Nation individuals living off-reserve in the midst of non-Aboriginal society.

In a sense, the Charter debate is now history. In Quebec, opposition to what René Lévesque called that "bloody Charter" (Cairns 1992a, 121) is now over, and Charter support in Quebec differs little from that among other Canadians (Bauch 2002; Fraser 2002). For Aboriginal peoples, the evidence of the debate being over may be more tentative. However, in a massive, exhaustive, and balanced recent survey of the status of Aboriginal peoples under the Charter, law professor Brad Morse noted that "the individual rights and liberties emphasized by the Charter are becoming more accepted and internalized by Aboriginal people," leading to challenges to laws and policies by any government, including Aboriginal governments. He also noted that Charter challenges to Aboriginal governments were leading to renewed discussion of the need to develop a rival Aboriginal charter (Morse, n.d., 62-63).

Constitutional Alienation and the Frustrations of Nationalism

Overall, the preceding catalogue of either opposition or half-hearted allegiance to the major institutions of the constitutional order adds up to a First Nations political culture of alienation/distrust/suspicion. From a First Nations perspective, the Canadian institutional environment is uncongenial; there is a misfit, difficult to measure, between First Nations aspirations and Canadian governing arrangements. In marked contrast, therefore, to newly independent Third World nations who were accommodated by and comfortably fitted into an expanding international state system, First Nations in Canada do not encounter a ready-made system of institutions appropriate to their ambitions and waiting to receive them.

Members of First Nations are uncertain citizens; the standard practice of representation in legislatures is considered inappropriate by many; Parliament's legitimacy is challenged; federalism is valued primarily for the opportunity a third order of government offers to escape the imposition of majority rule insensitive to the needs of indigenous nations; provincial governments tend to be viewed through suspicious eyes, and the Charter encounters significant opposition, even if it receives support from the Native Women's Association of Canada (Native Women's Association of Canada, n.d.).

It would be unwise to assume that the previous catalogue of antipathy to, simple lack of interest in, or lukewarm support for the major political institutions of the Canadian state is universally subscribed to by all or possibly even by a majority of individual members of First Nations.[69] It would be astonishing if there was not significant variation across the country or between on-reserve and off-reserve individuals.[70] However, when all the qualifications are listed and the probable diversity of views is underlined, the indisputable fact remains that there is a repudiation of, or distancing from, the core institutions of the Canadian state by a significant proportion of the First Nations population.

The frequently repeated assertion that indigenous peoples view self-determination as occurring within existing states (Barsh 1994, *passim*) undoubtedly applies to the Canadian situation. However, the amount of attention paid by the First Nation political elite and scholarly supporters of their position to the search for a viable political and constitutional arrangement with the non-Aboriginal majority is minimal compared to the effort and advocacy devoted to self-determination, self-government, and a third order of government. The limited emotional connection between First Nations and the institutions and practices of the constitutional order starkly underlines the magnitude of the task of developing/devising institutional meeting places where at least a limited acceptance of common membership in an overlapping civic community can emerge and grow. A rapprochement between First Nations and the Canadian state is a task of immense difficulty that will have to be pursued for decades, a pursuit in which a positive outcome is not guaranteed.

This rejectionism and alienation are historically rooted. They will not be significantly reduced or disappear in the short-term future. Memories of cultural stigmatization — residential schools (including language prohibition) and the banning of certain customs (potlatch, sun dance) — produce a distancing from the successors of those who sanctioned these cultural assaults. More generally, a colonial analysis of the past fosters the desire to achieve a community escape. Colonialism is an education in outsiderness. Its ending is more naturally seen in terms of self-government than in the incorporation and statistical disappearance of individuals in the Canadian community of citizens. This perspective is facilitated by the communal/territorial basis of over half of the First Nations population, which inevitably leads to a portrayal of a desirable future in terms of as much separate self-governing political existence as possible. This future vision is additionally supported and strengthened by the diffusion of the term "nation" throughout First Nation communities. Nation is simultaneously a servant of "otherness," an instrument of solidarity, and at the very least a competitor to Canadian citizenship.

Alienation from imperially imposed governing arrangements in Third World overseas colonies can be expressed in the choices available to the nationalist movement as it takes power, or shortly after, in a newly independent state. Often the initial choice, especially if the transfer of power has been peaceful, will be modelled on the constitutional and institutional arrangements of the mother country, which may turn out to be a temporary accommodation. The international system imposes fewer constraints of constitutional and institutional forms on newly independent Third World peoples than are imposed on Fourth World indigenous nations in polities with large settler majorities. These constraints are reinforced by the small population of the typical First Nation, which puts capacity limits on the jurisdictions that can be assumed.

The task confronting First Nation leaders and peoples and the governments and non-Aboriginal citizens of Canada is immense. The historical experience of First Nations, reinforced by the Third World example of former colonies emerging into independent statehood, supports a colonial interpretation of the past. That colonial analysis, however, unlike its Third World counterpart, founders when the question is not "Where have we been?" but "Where do we go from here?" The Third World trajectory of colonialism to independence is unavailable to Fourth World peoples. They have to seek a rapprochement within a common political system with the majority, whose predecessors were the instruments of their colonization.

DIFFICULTY OF ACHIEVING AN ACCOMMODATION: INCOMPATIBLE FUTURES?

Discussions of the direction in which we should be headed, of what moral meaning we should infuse into our inescapable geographical coexistence, of how much of a common civic identity we should aim for, are crucial questions which lack agreed-upon answers. Such explorations can range from the minute details of a child welfare agreement with a First Nation to larger questions of how we are to constitutionally relate to each other.

Helpful guidance in our search for answers to the latter question is provided by Charles Taylor, the distinguished Canadian philosopher. Taylor is only peripherally involved in the First Nations/Aboriginal debate, but he sets out in general terms two versions of a future set of relations which, when considered separately and then combined, move us in the direction of a necessary compromise. For students of Aboriginal issues, Taylor is usually encountered in terms of his "deep diversity" thesis, which is primarily directed to Quebec, and to a much lesser extent to Aboriginal peoples.[71] I will label the deep diversity Taylor, Taylor I. That discussion will be followed by a contrasting scenario, which I will call Taylor II. I begin with Taylor I: the deep diversity Taylor.

In *Shared and Divergent Values,* Taylor contrasted deep diversity with what he called "first-level diversity," which includes individuals of different culture, outlook, and background who nevertheless, partly via the Charter and multiculturalism, share "the same idea [as most Canadians] of what it is to belong to Canada." First-level diversity encompasses "new Canadians" drawn from all around the world following the liberalization of immigration criteria in the 1960s. They belong to Canada directly. However, for Quebecers, and for most French Canadians, the

> way of being Canadian ... is by their belonging to a constituent element of Canada.... Something analogous holds for aboriginal communities in this country;

their way of being Canadian is not accommodated by first-level diversity ... To build a country for everyone, Canada would have to allow for second-level or [what Taylor calls] "deep" diversity ... a Québécois or a Cree or a Dene might belong in a very different way, [by being] Canadian through being members of their national communities (Taylor 1993, 182-83).

The phrase "deep diversity" lends itself to misinterpretation. It does not necessarily translate into profound cultural divergence. For example, Taylor notes that in terms of values and political cultures, "English" Canada and French Canada are closer together than they have ever been. Cultural distance between immigrants who partake of first-level diversity and the society they enter is in many cases profoundly greater than the differences between English Canada and French Canada. In other words, on average, cultural diversity is much deeper in first-level diversity Canadians than for Taylor's prime deep-diversity community, Quebec or French Canada. "Deepness," to Taylor, resides in identity, in the sense of nationhood and the desire to continue as a separate people into the future. This is what singles out Quebec or French Canada — Taylor moves back and forth between the two conceptions — and Aboriginal nations. In its simplest form, for Taylor first-level diversity Canadians share a common patriotism, but not a common culture. Deep-diversity communities increasingly share a common culture but not a common patriotism. They are kept apart by competing senses of national belonging (Taylor 1993. Quote marks for "English" Canada are Taylor's.)

For Taylor I, members of deep-diversity communities will belong to Canada indirectly through their membership in a respected and recognized internal nation. They do not belong directly to Canada as citizens. Accordingly, internal deep-diversity nations will monopolize the allegiance of their members. The internal nation will be the intermediary between its individual members and the distant state of the country as a whole. The belonging to Canada of individuals in deep-diversity communities "pass[es] through their national communities" (Taylor 1993, 183; see also 199). To exaggerate only slightly, for internal deep diversity nations the overarching constitutional order will be more like a container than a focal point for citizen allegiance. Citizenship, in the sense of emotional belonging, will be located in the internal nations. The relationship with the pan-Canadian constitutional dimension is instrumental. As noted below, much of First Nations constitutional theorizing approximates Taylor I theorizing.

The Taylor I deep-diversity perspective, which is the view from below, is supplemented, if not contradicted by a very different Taylor II. In an article provocatively titled "Why Democracy Needs Patriotism (1996)," Taylor II argues that "strong identification on the part of their citizens" is a necessity in democratic societies, as is the belief "that their political society is a common venture of considerable moment." Contemporary democratic states, he asserts, need "a high degree of mobilization of their members, [which] occurs around common identities." Finally, "a high degree of mutual commitment" is necessary to sustain redistributive policies to reduce the alienation of minorities and the disadvantaged (Taylor 1996, 19-20).[72]

Taylor II appears to suggest that a comprehensive institutionalization of deep diversity will lead to a dangerous weakening of the capacity of the democratic state to implement policies for the alienated and less well-off. His argument, although perhaps not put quite so bluntly, is that deep diversity and a high degree of mutual commitment are uneasy partners. While Taylor II is clearly not arguing for a uniform undifferentiated citizenship, he is asserting that internal nations whose members are "in" but not "of" the larger society, whose members relate to the state in a Taylor I fashion, who view a common citizenship as an unacceptable instrument of assimilation are weakening the overall capacity of the state to enhance their welfare.[73]

Taylor I speaks to the nations within. He understands their desires. Taylor II speaks to federal and provincial governments; he understands the practical, functional considerations behind their desire to forge at least a limited version of a common civic community among all those who live within their borders. "Democratic states," he argues, "need something like a common identity" (Taylor 1999, 265; see also 271 and 272). In the absence of a common identity, he reluctantly observes, there is an understandable, albeit dangerous, temptation for the majority to exclude those who fall outside the identity which is natural and congenial to them.[74] This, of course, was the reality for reserve-based Indian peoples prior to the 1960 extension of the federal franchise. They were clearly excluded from common civic membership in the Canadian community. As a consequence, their overall public policy treatment was unquestionably inferior to that of the majority society, a discrepancy that became more pronounced and less defensible with the post-World War II development of the welfare state. Taylor II suggests that the avoidance of negative policy discrimination against minority communities/individuals is fostered by universal belonging to a common civic community. Taylor II argues that an uncompromising Taylor I approach may be seriously dysfunctional for the deep-diversity community it is supposed to advantage, unless the latter is rich in resources and governing capacity, which is rarely the case for the mostly small and all-too-often impoverished First Nations.

In spite of the preceding, First Nations and those who identify with their aspirations see an unadulterated Taylor II civic identity as too constricting, as disrespectful of their difference, and as a discordant reminder that historically they were excluded from earlier versions of an identity whose contemporary expression Taylor II appears to suggest that they should now embrace. A colonial analysis of the past, and the self-government goal to which it leads, inevitably views prospective constitutional arrangements in terms of the degree of self-determination, of distance from the pressures of the larger society which they offer.

Much of the language of First Nations nationalism in Canada leads in a Taylor I direction. Mary Ellen Turpel suggests that Aboriginal members of legislatures should be thought of as ambassadors (Turpel 1992, 600). The report of the RCAP clearly identifies "nations" as the constituent elements in the multinational Canada it advocates. That the Royal Commission paid minimal attention to Aboriginal political representation at the centre, and had a very weak conception of citizenship logically followed from the privileged position it accorded to the Aboriginal nation. Representation at the centre, which received only the cursory attention of a few pages in a five-volume report of over 3,500 pages, was to be by Aboriginal nations in a new third chamber with the task of acting as a watchdog on behalf of Aboriginal interests. There was no, or at least limited, indication that they would be participating in shared decisions that reflected a pan-Canadian dimension of their existence.

The RCAP report, therefore, can be described as a deep diversity document that paid negligible attention to the concerns of Taylor II. In slightly different language, the report looked at the Canadian future through the lens of Aboriginal, especially First Nation, desires, with minimal attention to what the Canadian community and its governments might see as desirable or achievable. Or again, from a federalism perspective the report focused on the self-rule (Taylor I) dimension and paid scant attention to the shared rule (Taylor II) dimension.

The report, it needs underlining, was the product of the most exhaustive inquiry of the Aboriginal past, present, and future ever undertaken. The commission had an Aboriginal majority — four of seven commissioners — and mounted an extraordinarily ambitious research program. Its recommendations and guiding philosophy can scarcely be described as idiosyncratic. They built on the emerging Aboriginal constitutional thought dating from the great awakening that followed the defeat of the 1969 White Paper.

In its more radical version, Aboriginal constitutional thought rejects the role of Canada in the life of First Nations. The recent Augustine-Richard Report on Burnt Church asserted that one group of band members "refuse to accept the authority of the Canadian government over their lives," deny "the legitimacy of Canada as a country," and claim to be a "sovereign people." The report noted that in some cases the appeal to nations can delegitimate the very idea of Canada. It suggested that the federal government's position "with respect to Aboriginal self-government is being perceived by some First Nation communities to extend to total political independence." The caution followed that the Canadian government should make it clear that the "territorial integrity" of Canada is not bargainable (Augustine and Richard 2002, 8, 24 and 30-1; see also Simpson 2002).[75] Burnt Church is probably not typical, but neither is it unique. RCAP observed that "in many cases" Aboriginal nations deny that Canada's sovereignty applies to them (Canada 1996, vol. 1, 608). Further, as previously noted, there is extensive alienation from the Canadian constitutional order, with sporadic denials by individuals that they are Canadian citizens and descriptions of those who are as "uncertain citizens" (Borrows 2001).

First Nations constitutional thought and that of their supporters concentrates on the maximum escape possible from the past, on exit. The goal is as much of a Third World solution as is possible. Nation has a stronger presence in their vocabulary than *citizenship*. Their academic supporters argue for a distinct treaty order of federalism outside the federal-provincial order. James Tully, one of the leading exponents of this position, describes the view that Aboriginal peoples are part of the "federal-provincial confederation" as "a travesty of history." He proposes a reconceptualization of Canada as comprising two separate confederations: the federal-provincial one familiar to all students and a treaty confederation of "First Nations with the Crown and later with the federal and, to some extent provincial governments." Canada then becomes "a political association of two confederations" (Tully 1999, 424-25). The relationship is variously described as "nation-to-nation," as "side-by-side," and as a "partnership" (ibid., 419, 423 and 424).[76]

Treaty federalism, in which treaties rather than citizenship are the bonding mechanism, in effect proposes to internationalize the domestic system, and has only a weak answer to the question of what is to be the source of cohesion.[77] The frequently referred to "two-row-wampum" vision of two societies travelling in separate ships down the river of life, with an agreed mutual respect for each other's autonomy, suggests at best a tolerant coexistence, but negligible interest in the idea of a common society.[78] This pattern of thinking is profoundly rooted in the historical experience of First Nations. Its origins are similar to the origins of Third World independence-seeking nationalism — regrettably constrained in the Fourth World by the reality that a similar independence outcome is not possible. The overall impression is of Indian nations/peoples being in, but not of, the surrounding society. If federalism is about self-rule and shared rule, the colonized, especially if they combine territory and governing authority as First Nations do, will focus their attention on self-rule, in the Canadian case on a third order of government. Shared rule, which is normally buttressed by a common citizenship in standard federal systems, will get limited attention.[79]

Surely, if the entire First Nations population were positioned in another Nunavut with an adequate resource base, independence would be pursued, if not already achieved. It is a "regrettable necessity," as Joseph Carens observes, (Carens 2000, 173) that precludes independence. Would Ovide Mercredi have said, "we know we cannot displace the alien government completely ... the objective is to live together," (Mercredi and Turpel 1993, 198) if three-quarters of a million First Nations people were an overwhelming majority in a bounded and resource-rich territory? However, Mercredi and Carens are not responding to the wishes of a concentrated reasonably large and economically prosperous population, but on the whole, to scattered enclaves of poor and small populations. Fleras and Maaka's observation clearly applies to Canada: "In structural terms, most indigenous peoples occupy an encapsulated status as disempowered and dispersed subjects of a larger political entity" (Fleras and Maaka 2000, 114).

That larger political entity is driven by its own internal logic, which Taylor also understands. In marked contrast to his deep-diversity thesis, with its sympathetic focus on internal nations seeking outlets to express and sustain their historically-based differences of culture and identity, Taylor II argues for the need for democratic states to be able to call on the loyalty and identity of their citizenry for major public policies. In a sense he has simply changed his vantage point. Taylor I focused on the desire of internal nations to maximize their escape from the smothering embrace of the larger society, including a rejection of individual citizen membership in the pan-Canadian community. Taylor II's focus is on the overall government of the larger society and the requirements for its effective functioning.

In general, historic states with indigenous nations within their borders will opt for a version of Taylor II. They will seek to limit departures from their view of normality in the constitutional order. The 1969 White Paper was a classic example of a strong version of Taylor II, as was historic Indian policy with its goal of enfranchisement.

Federal and provincial governments seek an accommodation that is compatible with (a modified version of) the inherited constitutional order, which means generally compatible with institutions rejected or distrusted by many First Nations.[80] They do not see themselves either as imperialists or as the successors of imperialists. Hence, their policies do not envision a form of coexistence in which parallel societies exist side-by-side in separate compartments. They insist that the Charter must apply. They display no interest in the kind of Aboriginal watchdog third House proposed by RCAP. Federal and provincial government positions are no less natural to them than the constitutional thought of First Nations is to successive National Chiefs of the AFN. The premise behind federal policy is that the members of Aboriginal peoples/ nations may not be citizens like the others, but they are Canadian citizens. The federal position is that "citizenship is the institutional arrangement that makes empathy a natural fellow-feeling for all within its compass" (Cairns 1999*a*, 5.) However, as I have argued elsewhere, in a Taylor I situation, the "capacity of citizenship to sustain empathy for all members of the polity is reduced, and the capacity of the central authorities to employ citizenship as a resource is diminished" (ibid., 8).

First Nations preference for Taylor I is logical and natural. Taylor I speaks sympathetically to their colonized past. Taylor II also speaks sympathetically to the equally natural tendency of federal and provincial governments to claim and foster some degree of direct unmediated allegiance of the individuals, peoples, nations within their borders.

WHERE DOES THIS LEAVE US?

At the extremes, Taylor I and Taylor II are not only incompatible with each other, they are each unworkable in the Canadian setting. Evidence is clear that First Nations will not accept any uncompromising version of Taylor II. Not only would such an outcome be viewed as a return to the White Paper, as a point of fact the constitutional protection of Aboriginal and treaty rights in section 35 of the *Constitution Act, 1982* precludes it.

On the other hand, Taylor I is also problematic. First Nations on average are too small, and the jurisdictions they can wield are too limited for the quasi-separate existence visualized by deep-diversity relations.[81] I have already argued that the "immensely ambitious and arduous project" of maintaining what Kymlicka describes as "a separate societal culture in a modern state" (Kymlicka 1998, 31) is beyond the capacity of First Nations. The federal and provincial governments are too important for the future of small First Nations for their members to be involved only as nations and not as citizens in the political process at federal and provincial levels. In any event, there is negligible likelihood that the federal and provincial governments would agree to deep-diversity relations with anywhere from 60 to 80, to over 600 distinct First Nation communities which would geographically be within Canada, but whose individual members would not have a significant degree of direct citizen relations with federal and provincial Canada. While Taylor I is not available as a realistic choice, any pure version of Taylor II has been repudiated by First Nations nationalism and by the political developments of the last 40 years.

Let us consider some observations by four sets of authors, including Taylor, that will help to give us a sense of direction in this debate.

The task, according to Taylor, is to share "identity space," creatively working out new "political identities ... between peoples who have to or want to live together under the same political roof (and this coexistence is always grounded in some mixture of necessity and choice)" (Taylor 1999, 281).[82]

The massive nature of the enterprise of generating a togetherness that is not smothering and a separateness that is not isolating includes what Cameron and Wherrett call a "shift in the paradigm of social and political reality in which we all live ... [which will require] a redefinition of the origin and nature of the majority society as well as ... address[ing] the circumstances of Aboriginal nations and communities." This quest ultimately leads the majority society to "a reconsideration of [its] history ... of assumptions about sovereignty and conventional government structures, and the very vocabulary [employed] ... to describe significant dimensions of [its] social and political world" (Cameron and Wherrett 1995, 92).[83]

Taylor and Cameron and Wherrett are saying the same thing, which is that we need to rethink "who we are" in the new circumstances of First Nations nationalism. Taylor put it nicely: the majority has to move to a "looser 'us' to accommodate 'them'"[84] (Taylor 2001, 4).

Fleras and Maaka, writing about New Zealand, identify the fundamental issue that confronts settler societies with indigenous minority nations: "Will the extension of indigeneity as principle and practice create a society that is bifurcated around two constitutionalisms, thus creating new forms of segregation?" The challenge of constitutional transformation, accordingly, "lies in acknowledging [indigenous peoples'] rights as original occupants and political communities, without undermining societal cohesion and national identity in the process" (Fleras and Maaka 2000, 119).

John Borrows, a First Nations Chippewa scholar, recently and passionately argued for full and committed Aboriginal participation in Canadian affairs on the grounds that self-government in small communities was a limited goal. He cited high rates of intermarriage, significant breakthroughs in postsecondary education and large indigenous populations without a land base, many in urban settings, as evidence of a high degree of interdependence. Aboriginal participation in the major Canadian public and private institutions was essential if that interdependence was to be more than a one-way street. "Aboriginal control of Aboriginal affairs" by self-government for small communities was not enough (Borrows 1999, 74-80).

The composite set of instructions that emerges from the preceding is that the majority must move toward a more generous and inclusive interpretation of *we*, and that rejection by First Nations of a tolerant version of inclusion will result in a coexistence with a diluted empathy and solidarity. An inward-looking First Nation nationalism focusing on self-government within small communities contributes to a truncated non-Aboriginal *we*, disconnected from First Nation lives. It also contributes to a truncated First Nations' *we* that has difficulty accommodating indigenous peoples without a land base, often in urban settings. A constitutional future fashioned on a domestic version of an international system in which the units are nations interacting with each other will not work. Equally, an assertive, historic definition of a non-Aboriginal *we* fashioned before First Nations emerged from the sidelines is no less unpromising.

CONCLUSION

What Bhikhu Parekh says of multicultural societies is even truer of multinational societies. They "throw up problems that have no parallel in history, ... political unity without cultural uniformity," inclusiveness without assimilation, reconciliation of "a common sense of belonging while respecting ... legitimate cultural differences, and cherishing plural cultural identities without weakening the shared and precious identity of shared citizenship" (Parekh 2000, 343).

In making sense of where we are in the complex policy area involving the struggle of indigenous peoples to escape from a colonized past, we have to position ourselves in the broad sweep of domestic and global history. This does not mean, of course, that we are blind puppets of historical forces. It does mean, however, that we should look outward at what is happening elsewhere. We are not alone. We should also look backward; where we are has a history.

Policymakers have to grapple with two powerful forces: indigenous nationalism and the inherited state form. Nationalism is one of the most powerful mobilizing vehicles of the contemporary era. It generates an introspective solidarity among First Nations which, in the Canadian case, is accompanied by a profound constitutional alienation. It encounters the Canadian state, well into its second century, perhaps battered by globalization, but showing no signs of disappearance. The state is here to stay. Employing the resources of nationalism and patriotism, it has a remarkable capacity to mobilize the people over whom it wields authority.

The resulting conflict of nationalisms is frustrating to both. Indigenous nationalism is frustrated by its inability to follow the Third World development path to independence. It is doubly frustrated by the fact that the governing capacity of small populations, best thought of as mini-nations, with average populations under 500, is limited. The Canadian state is frustrated by its inability to generate the civic identities it considers essential to its long-run functioning. Given these realities, the fact that a grand reconciliation is not on our immediate horizon is not surprising.

Many dozens of states face similar concerns: how to work out a rapprochement between indigenous populations and the majority population and the inherited institutional/constitutional configurations of the latter. From the indigenous perspective, some 300 million indigenous people struggle in those states to leave colonialism behind and work out a way of living together with the successors of the colonizers. From the states' perspectives, particularly when indigenous numbers are proportionately small, acceptable terms of reconciliation will modify and supplement inherited constitutional arrangements without derailing them.

In Canada we are in the midst of an unfolding experiment of refashioning the Canadian state. An old order which had prevailed for much of the modern era in which indigenous peoples were marginalized, despoiled of their lands, culturally assaulted, and often experienced cataclysmic population declines is on the defensive. The demise of a hierarchically structured relationship has been announced, while the search for its successor is underway. It would be reassuring if we could report a consensual statement about the detailed goals toward which we should be heading, and precisely how to get there, but we cannot. The BC Treaty Commission, looking back on almost ten years of disappointing results flowing from its efforts to facilitate treaty-making — no treaties have been finalized — observed the lack of a "common understanding of the parameters and fundamental goals of treaty negotiations ... In some cases First Nations have an unclear vision about their own futures ... More problematic are the conflicting messages delivered by the governments of Canada and BC as to their goals in treaty making" (BC Treaty Commission 2002*a*, 17; see also 6).[85] This lack of a common agreement on a future that is both desirable and attainable is typical of the countries in which the indigenous peoples of the world are scattered.[86]

This may be troubling, but it is not surprising. We are caught in the Canadian version of a global movement of indigenous Fourth World peoples no longer willing to be left on the sidelines while others provide the sense of direction. This global movement builds on the Third World's successful assault on western imperialism, resulting in more than a hundred new states and a transformed international system. The Fourth World, however, possibly with a few exceptions, cannot follow the Third World example of independence. In each locale a reconciliation has to be worked out that will facilitate a version of a common community without smothering minority internal nations. Alternatively phrased, the necessary and desirable creation of constitutional space for minority nations has to be accommodated to the understandable desire of the majority and existing governments to have a significant degree of across-the-board commonality in an unmediated relationship between individuals and the state. The natural vehicle for this is citizenship.

Neither Taylor I, nor Taylor II — seen as separate options — provides an acceptable, viable answer. Each must bend to the other to create a middle ground in which constitutional recognition of indigenous diversity is accompanied by what is perhaps best described as an overlapping citizenship regime, or differentiated citizenship. The latter is not separate citizenships, but a citizenship in which some, but not all components of citizenship are shared, and some but not all components are different. What this means in practical terms has to be worked out on a case-by-case basis in circumstances where the successors of the colonized and the colonizers have, in some sense, to live together.

The ending of overseas colonialism in the Third World was epochal. It changed the human map of relations among peoples, and dramatically transformed the international system. The end of internal colonialism in the Fourth World will be only slightly less so. We are refashioning the domestic constitutional and institutional relations of the society and political community in which indigenous minorities live. We are reinventing the meaning of statehood. The ending of internal colonialism is much more complicated than ending the overseas variety. The "natural" positions of the contending parties, governments and majority populations sitting across the bargaining table from First Nations, approach the task of constitution-making from divergent perspectives. First Nations, responding to the experience of colonization, seek the maximum viable exit possible from a polity which, at least in its earlier version, was the instrument of their wardship, marginalization, dispossession, and stigmatization. They also seek redress: a Canadian Truth Commission may be appropriate.[87] Given this background, it is understandable that "First Nation" has a more prominent place in the indigenous vocabulary than "citizen." The goal of self-government takes priority over participation in federal and provincial legislatures. Federal (and provincial) governments, by contrast, naturally stress the Canadian dimension. Parekh observes that "the modern state is suspicious of, and feels threatened by, well-organized ethnic, religious and other communities lest they should mediate the relations between it and the citizen and set up rival foci of loyalty" (Parekh 2000, 182). They seek at least a significant degree of overlap between belonging to a First Nation and belonging to Canada. By the latter, they mean some version of a common citizenship — so that there is an inclusive *we*. Critics may view this as an indication of an unthinking constitutional conservatism that is unable/ unwilling to see a reliance on treaties as an adequate instrument to support the degree of solidarity that sustains our reciprocal responsibility for each other. I disagree, by expressing the caution that there are functional limits to the institutionalization of diversity for small and poor self-governing peoples/ nations that are set by the requirement of an embracing commonality which sustains reciprocal empathy for each other. Charles Taylor puts it well in asserting that we must not let our pursuit of one good "lead us to undervalue, or even lose from sight, important virtues of society, goals like social harmony, a sense of solidarity, mutual understanding and a sense of civility, which we neglect at our peril" (Taylor 2001, 4).[88]

The goal, therefore, is reasonably clear — to work toward a solution sympathetic to the anti-colonialism that motivates First Nations and the desire for a distinctive place and constitutional recognition to which it leads on the one hand, and the requirement of the Canadian state for an allegiance to the constitutional order not entirely mediated by First Nation membership.[89] The goal might be phrased as institutionalizing a compromise between Taylor I and Taylor II. While this compromise will not be easily achieved, it has its virtues. It is more achievable than the extremes it straddles — the view that pushes toward the White Paper and a relatively undifferentiated citizenship, and the counter view, which sees Canada as an aggregation of treaty-linked quasi-solitudes. The first is unacceptable for good reasons to First Nations. The second is unacceptable for good reasons to the federal and provincial governments and to the non-Aboriginal population. In contrast to the alternatives, this necessary compromise has some prospect of long-run viability.

Those who suggest or imply that a reconstitutionalized Canada can survive as a multinational polity with dozens, perhaps hundreds of nations ranging from a few thousand to the 30 million nation of non-Aboriginal Canada, linked by treaties but with negligible common citizenship bonds are obligated to show the viability of their proposals.[90] Those who argue that the White Paper had the correct vision for the future, in which citizenship is all, and First Nations are accorded museum status are obligated to show that their vision can roll back Aboriginal nationalism and that section 35 of the *Constitution Act, 1982* can be bypassed.

I do not believe that even the most passionate supporter of the above alternative road maps to the future can successfully defend them as attainable and viable over time. My position is that Charles Taylor got it right if we can blend Taylor I and Taylor II into a composite vision.

POSTSCRIPT: A RECIPE FOR LIVING TOGETHER

In its original version, this paper ended with the previous paragraph. However, two readers suggested that a concluding section spelling out what a hybrid of Taylor I and Taylor II would look like would strengthen the paper. In other words, what arrangements for living together could respond to the Aboriginal desire for constitutional space to accommodate self-determination within

Canada (Taylor I), and also to the interests of the Canadian state in a version of civic belonging, to a possibly modified version of citizenship that would incorporate Indian, Inuit, and Métis individuals as members of the pan-Canadian community (Taylor II).

The readers' suggestion was a tall order. I rejected the possibility that my response should include a detailed discussion of a division of powers for three orders of government, although that issue is addressed at a general level. In the following pages, the focus is at a macro level, verging on an exercise in constitutional theory. (See Abele and Prince 2003 for a more grounded approach.) As noted immediately below, we are not alone in having difficulty finding a stable accommodation/reconciliation between indigenous nations and the country-wide nationalism of the states in which they live.

One final preliminary observation: my focus is on First Nations living on their own territories. Hence, although "Aboriginal" is frequently used, little attention is given to Inuit and Métis. Further, the large off-reserve population receives limited attention, although elsewhere I have argued that its neglect contributes to an urban Aboriginal underclass that threatens social stability in major urban centres in western Canada (Cairns 2000c). However, the attempt to think clearly about the relationship between the Canadian state and the nationalism of land-based First Nations is enough of a challenge for a postscript.

The reconciliation of a version of Taylor I and Taylor II is a requirement for all states confronting internal indigenous nations. The latter seek some degree of civic commonality embracing all who are subject to their governance. The former, wounded by colonialism, seek to take as much control of their future by self-government as is possible. They see escape from a colonial past as the collective emancipation of a nation, not as separate citizen memberships in the community of their former oppressors. In Canada, indigenous nations deprived of the possibility of independence, do not see standard individual membership in the Canadian community of citizens as an adequate response to their existence as nations. Representatives of the Canadian federal state, however, driven by the (perceived) necessity of a positive connection with all who live within its borders, insist that Aboriginal nations and their citizens are subject to a host of Canadian requirements (described below). A hybrid of Taylor I and II is an attempt to bridge these competing visions. The question is: How do we constitutionally and practically respect a flourishing indigenous diversity and simultaneously maintain social cohesion (see Borrows 2003, 226 and 229-32)?

The contestation between indigenous nationalism and the encircling civic nationalism of the state is not unique to Canada. A recent special issue of *Citizenship Studies* which focused on "Aboriginal Citizenship" in various countries provided few grounds for optimism that a reconciliation is on the horizon. The various authors described a constitutional stalemate in the clashes between indigenous nationalisms and the states in which indigenous peoples struggle to escape from their colonized past (*Citizenship Studies* 2003). The overall tenor of the country studies, and the related literature on which they drew, was a stark pessimism. Augie Fleras, writing in another volume comparing indigenous peoples' rights in Canada, Australia, and New Zealand, asserted that we are trapped in "a messy paradigm 'muddle.' Indigenous-State relations are imbued with an air of ambivalence as colonialist paradigms grind up against post-colonial realities" (Fleras 1999, 227). Ned Franks, writing of Canada in yet another comparative volume — this time dealing with Canada, the United States, Mexico, and Latin America — repeated Fleras' pessimism by referring to "a seemingly unbridgeable chasm ... between the aspirations of Aboriginal leaders [in Canada] and what other levels of government are willing to grant" (Franks 2000, 113; see also Abele and Prince 2003, 137 and *passim*).

McDonnell and Depew locate the conflict that resists resolution in the clash between the cultural rootedness of self-determination in particular indigenous communities, and the abstract bureaucratic requirements of the Canadian state. "The space," they write, "for [self-determination] to occur must be found within the judicial and administrative apparatus of the modern state." Unfortunately, self-government negotiations, they argue, have been dominated by the state's bureaucratic concerns which have vanquished grassroots Aboriginal input, to the detriment of successful negotiated outcomes. The general tenor of self-government negotiations "has been in the direction of cutting Aboriginal people down to size, which is to say down to a size imagined as manageable by the state"(McDonnell and Depew 1999, 353).[91]

It is difficult to find grounds for optimism either in comparative studies of indigenous-state relations, or in the history of failed attempts at major change in those relations in Canada: the withdrawn 1969 White Paper, the minuscule progress achieved by four constitutional conferences on Aboriginal concerns (1983–87), the defeated Charlottetown Accord (1993), the limited impact of the report of the Royal Commission on Aboriginal Peoples (1996), and the rise and fall of the recent *Governance Act* (Canada. Minister of Indian Affairs and Northern Development 2002).

Indeed, Andy Scott, the newly appointed minister of indian affairs, had scarcely assumed his new portfolio when he indicated to no one's surprise that the *Governance Act* introduced in the closing years of the Chrétien regime would not be reintroduced, and then gloomily asserted: "My colleagues, and generally Canadians, are uncertain as to whether anything can be done or what can be done" about socio-economic disparities between natives and non-natives. "There's a sense of pessimism in terms of this file," he concluded (Lunman 2004). Given the preceding, optimism would be Panglossian.

However, in the Canadian case a despairing pessimism would be an overreaction. There are resources in our recent past, particularly the *Constitution Act, 1982* which, with all their imperfections, at least point us in the right direction and provide some grounds for limited hope. In the next few pages, I will look at the 1982 act and the federal government's self-government negotiating position to see if they are building blocks of a reasonable hybrid of Taylor I and II.

The combination of the Charter, including the section 25 qualification to its application to Aboriginal peoples, and section 35 of the *Constitution Act, 1982* constitutes a possible bridge between Taylor I and Taylor II. The fact that the Charter, with its notwithstanding clause, was a compromise between the federal government and several provincial opponents of the Trudeau vision is a given. Less noticed is the compromise between the Charter and the rights of Aboriginal nations.

Section 25 of the *Canadian Charter of Rights and Freedoms* states that:

> The guarantee in this Charter of certain rights and freedoms shall not be construed so as to abrogate or derogate from any aboriginal, treaty or other rights or freedoms that pertain to the aboriginal peoples of Canada, including
> (a) any rights or freedoms that have been recognized by the Royal Proclamation of October 7, 1763; and
> (b) any rights or freedoms that now exist by way of land claims agreements or may be so acquired.

Section 25 is an "interpretive prism" to prevent a reading of the Charter that would undermine Aboriginal rights. It is, therefore, a protective instrument (Morse 1999*b*, 19).

The Charter is now generally recognized as a nation-building instrument, originally designed to strengthen Canadian identities against centrifugal provincialism and Québécois nationalism, especially of the *indépendentiste* variety. This political purpose explains both the original federal government sponsorship of the Charter, and the provincial government opposition, particularly of Quebec, Saskatchewan, and Manitoba (Cairns 1992*b*). That same Canadian nation-building purpose explains the original opposition to the Charter of the Assembly of First Nations (First Nations Circle on the Constitution 1992, 68) and of scholars sympathetic to Aboriginal nationalism. From the AFN perspective, the Charter was correctly seen as an instrument of a rival nationalism. While, as previously noted, the Charter is now taking root among First Nations, a result that may be seen positively by the heirs of the Trudeau vision, others continue to see the Charter as a threat to the integrity of First Nation societies.

The Charter, with its purpose of strengthening identification with the Canadian constitutional order by the vehicle of rights, is a classic example of Taylor II. Simultaneously, the section 25 qualification of the Charter's application so as not "to abrogate or derogate from any Aboriginal, treaty or other rights or freedoms" reflects, at least modestly, a Taylor I perspective, which receives a more emphatic recognition of a Taylor I commitment to support for deep diversity in section 35 of the *Constitution Act, 1982*.

Section 35 states that: "The existing aboriginal and treaty rights of the aboriginal peoples of Canada are hereby recognized and affirmed." The original section 35 is supplemented by a 1983 amendment, which states that "for greater certainty ... 'treaty rights' includes rights that now exist by way of land claims agreements or may be so acquired." These section 35 clauses constitutionalize a version of the Taylor I position. On its face, section 35 is an instrument of decolonization and constitutional affirmation, both, of course, within Canada. The combination of the Charter, the section 25 exception to its application, and the rights affirmations of section 35, clearly express a hybrid or blending of Taylor I and II. This compromise is now part of our constitutional philosophy. Canadians are constitutionally committed by these instruments to coexisting nation-building projects — for the country as a whole via the Charter, and to Aboriginal nation-building as the decolonization consequences of section 35 are fleshed out by, *inter alia*, judicial decisions, and new treaties/agreements.

This package of constitutional changes, now in its third decade, is a major achievement. It encompasses a fundamental criterion of contemporary Canadian statehood, the Charter, and a central goal of indigenous nationalism — a constitutionally protected recognition of Aboriginal and treaty rights, albeit the comprehensive translation of the latter into specific enforceable rights is a project still underway. It remains, however, a flawed achievement, with one legal scholar asserting "compelling legal arguments for concluding that, apart from the gender equality provision in section 28, the Charter does not apply to ... Aboriginal governments" (McNeil 2001*a*, 247-48). Cultural arguments are also employed to delegitimize the Charter. Dan Russell contrasted Aboriginal values and Charter rights, and argued that the Charter has the capacity to undermine Aboriginal customs and culture. In *A People's Dream*, he canvassed various options, including the suggestion that the Charter would apply to Aboriginal communities until they adopt their own charters. If this has not occurred "after five years, ... then the Canadian Charter would become the permanent community charter" (Russell 2000, 123 and 144). While this is a plausible proposal, its implementation would reopen the debates about the Charter's applicability and appropriateness that were deeply divisive and wounding in native communities (Borrows 1994, 21 and 31). As Schouls points out, based on a reading of transcripts of the RCAP hearings, there are passionate supporters of the Charter, especially among Native women and youth (Schouls 2003, 93; see also 100-05 and 167-71).[92] Further, if Russell's proposal was taken up on a widespread basis, it would remove the opting-out of First Nations from the orbit of a constitutional instrument that has come to define "Canadianness." The likelihood of the federal government supporting such a development is infinitesimal. It could lead to a Charter checkerboard which almost certainly would be deemed deeply offensive to the Charter Canadians who contributed to the demise of the Meech Lake Accord, which they believed threatened "their Charter."[93]

Given the complexity and volatility of the issue, the more modest proposals of the Charlottetown Accord deserve consideration. Aboriginal peoples should be consulted by provincial and territorial governments when candidates are proposed to fill Supreme Court vacancies, and Aboriginal groups should have the right to make their own representations for membership on the Supreme Court. Finally, and intriguingly, the Accord recommended consultation between the federal government and Aboriginal groups on the "proposal that an Aboriginal Council of Elders be entitled to make submissions to the Supreme Court when the court considers Aboriginal issues" (Cited in Russell 2000, 181).[94]

These Charlottetown proposals, which were only a small part of the overall Accord, have the virtue of preserving the Charter's role in strengthening Canadians' identification with the constitution, while simultaneously sensitizing the Charter's interpretation to Aboriginal values and concerns. Accordingly, these proposed indirect modifications of the process of Charter interpretation are examples of a nuanced Taylor II, the necessity for the state to strengthen its positive and direct rapport with a society composed of more than one people.

Supreme Court adjudication of the Charter needs to be sensitive to Aboriginal concerns. The Charter, qualified by section 25, and interpreted by a Supreme Court whose role and membership are influenced by the Charlottetown proposals just described, is a reasonable balance between Taylor I and II.

Moving to questions of jurisdiction, it is clear from federal government position papers and its bargaining posture in treaty negotiations that the great affairs of state will remain in federal (and provincial) hands. The 1995 federal government policy statement on Aboriginal self-government contains a lengthy list of subjects where there is no compelling reason for "Aboriginal governments or institutions to exercise law-making authority," including subject matters related to sovereignty, defence and external relations, and "other national interest powers," such as management of the national economy, national law and order, health and safety, and specific federal undertakings such as aeronautics and the postal service (see Morse 1999*b*, 33 for extensive listing and discussion). These declarations and the lengthy federal list of untouchables confirm the limits to self-government. This position is reasserted in the federal statement that no departure will be allowed "from the basic principle that those federal and provincial laws of overriding national or provincial importance will prevail over conflicting Aboriginal laws" (Irwin 1995, 11; see also McNeil 2001*b*, 176-77 for discussion of analogous provisions in the Charlottetown Accord).

The federal (and provincial) dominance of the great affairs of state contrasts with the jurisdiction of Aboriginal governments that will likely extend "to matters that are internal to the group, integral to its distinct Aboriginal culture, and essential to its operation as a government or institution" (Irwin 1995, 5; see Morse 1999*b*, 31-32 for an extensive listing of what this might encompass).

It should not be forgotten that there are other (semi) official descriptions of the potential sphere of Aboriginal governance, most notably that of RCAP and the Charlottetown Accord. Indeed, Russell notes with some astonishment that the RCAP proposals are much more limiting than the prior Charlottetown Accord proposals which had received the support of all governments of the federal system and of the major Aboriginal organizations. The Accord not only significantly extended Aboriginal exemptions from the Charter, but provided Aboriginal input into "virtually every major institution of the Canadian state" (Cairns 2000*a*, 83) and generously described Aboriginal governments' jurisdiction. The *Consensus Report* described the rationale for Aboriginal governments' authority as being "(a) to safeguard and develop their languages, cultures, economies, identities, institutions and traditions; and, (b) to develop, maintain and strengthen their relationship with their lands, waters and environment so as to determine and control their development as peoples according to their own values and priorities and ensure the integrity of their societies" (cited in Cairns 2000*a*, 83; see 81-84 for a summary of the Accord; see also McNeil 2001*a*).

The accordion-like quality of changing descriptions over time of Aboriginal governments' possible jurisdiction indicates that this is contested territory, that in the right circumstances Taylor I is capable of expansion. The potential jurisdiction of self-government is indeterminate. There is immense variation in the jurisdictional proposals from the Penner Report (1983), to Charlottetown, to the 1995 federal government position paper, to RCAP. This area, therefore, is unsettled territory, with the existing federal position more restrictive than some of the previous proposals. In the right circumstances, therefore, the jurisdictional response to Aboriginal nationalism (Taylor I) may exceed the existing federal proposals.

In terms of *realpolitick*, however, the upper limits to Aboriginal self-government are set not only by federal policy, but also by the limited governing capacity of small populations and by land and resource limitations (see Harris 2002, ch. 9 for powerful advocacy of more generous land allocation for First Nations in BC). Since the constraints of small populations have been presented elsewhere in this monograph, they do not need to be elaborated here, except as a reminder that over a hundred bands have on-reserve populations of less than one hundred, and nearly two-thirds of First Nations have on-reserve populations of less than 500, discouraging realities that are frequently overlooked or masked behind the "nation" label.[95]

It is undoubtedly true that contemporary small band populations reflect the fragmenting effects of federal policy on the original indigenous 60–80 nations (RCAP's estimate) which pre-existed the arrival of Europeans. The contemporary reality, however caused, nevertheless remains for the small populations just described.[96] Some consolidations may be stimulated by federal incentives, but such consolidations are unlikely to be the norm. More generally, as McDonnell and Depew emphasize, RCAP's language of nation applied to the future results of band consolidations is "a dangerously naive strategy," which ignores the complexity of many communities. It suggests that the "commission does not know what identities, languages, spiritualities, and so forth may have to be collapsed or coalesced to provide a nation unit with that complement of human resources [the commission considers] sufficient to exercise negotiated self-government responsibilities" (McDonnell and Depew 1999, 357).

Consolidations will only occur in atypical circumstances, and even when they do, the population numbers will still hover around village size. For the foreseeable future, therefore, self-governing First Nations will have small populations. Cultural differences, geography, the history of living together in the existing small communities, and the self-interest of governing chiefs and councils set limits to amalgamations to produce larger communities. The tasks that Aboriginal communities can handle will be dictated as much by small-ness as by federal policy. Even a more sensitive Supreme Court, a more generous interpretation of section 35, and fewer constraints on the jurisdic-tion of self-governing Aboriginal nations would confront the effective limitations on self-government set by the small size of Aboriginal communi-ties and, in most cases, the limited resources at their disposal.

Accordingly, a central task for supporters of self-government is to search for ways to enhance the governing capacities of First Nations. This means producing a cadre of skilled administrators, finding ways that several First Nations can cooperate in purchasing services where feasible, and, while not forgetting McDonnell and Depew's cautionary observations, increased resort to tribal councils and amalgamations where possible of First Nations to pro-duce more viable populations. Future projections of what is possible should be governed by the extent that population and resource limitations are remov-able, the exploration of which should be one of the most high priority tasks of supporters of self-government.[97]

The limited version just described of a partial compromise between Taylor I and Taylor II — the Charter qualified by section 25, by the rights and recognitions of section 35, and the 1995 federal government policy position on jurisdictions available for self-governing nations, which in effect is a pro-posal for a future division of powers — may not survive the politics of the future struggles between Aboriginal peoples and the Canadian state. This pack-age reflects an implicit blending of Taylor I, support for internal Aboriginal nations, and Taylor II, support for the Canadian state's desire for a compre-hensive embrace of all within its borders. While our successors may look back on this package as one more of the many gods that have failed in this fraught policy area, it remains a huge step forward, light years away from the decades prior to 1982. Nevertheless, its weaknesses need to be further identified, some of which relate to the federal government's position paper on self-government, and others to section 35. The former is correctly characterized by Michael Murphy as revealing "troubling elements of unilateralism. The government established, at the outset, the scope of policy jurisdictions that were open to negotiation, and dictated a set of financial, administrative and democratic benchmarks that Aboriginal governments were required to meet in order to exercise the right to self-government" (Murphy 2004, 158).

A recent collection of essays on section 35 was overwhelmingly critical (see McNeil 2001*c* and Borrows 2002*b*). By nearly all accounts, section 35 has failed to live up to its initial promise. Indeed, contrary to its clear word-ing, it has become a vehicle for restricting rather than respecting Aboriginal

rights (Borrows 2003, 247; see also Walkem 2003, 216).[98] One group of authors, the optimists, thought it might still be salvaged. A second group,
pessimistic about its current interpretation, sought a "fundamental transformation" of its interpretation "that will acknowledge and respect Indigenous
Peoples as Nations with both territorial and law-making jurisdiction equal (or
roughly so) to those of Canada." A third group sought to go beyond section 35
with the goal of nation-to-nation relationships outside the Canadian constitution (Walkem and Bruce 2003, 11-12).

Since this paper is organized around the premise that the future relationship between Aboriginal nations and the Canadian state will be dictated more
by practical concerns than by the more radical nationalist aspirations, such as
acknowledgement and respect for "Indigenous Peoples as Nations with both
territorial and law-making jurisdiction equal (or nearly so) to those of Canada,"
or nation-to-nation relationships outside the Canadian constitution — the hybrid of Taylor I and II is best served by a more generous, less restrictive
interpretation of section 35, which should be understood as an instrument of
decolonization.

Viewed through the criteria of balance and as a hybrid of Taylor I and II
the Aboriginal clauses of the *Constitution Act, 1982* and the federal government policy position on self-government represents a distinct improvement
over the pre-1982 era. Nevertheless, this existing attempted reconciliation of
Aboriginal nationalism and the Canadian state is flawed. As noted above, the
compromise tilts too heavily on the federal side.

A major weakness of the vast literature on rights, on self-government,
and on what should be done in the area of Aboriginal-state relations in Canada
is the negligible attention to how Aboriginal peoples are to relate to the representative political institutions of the country in which they live. This is
especially true of writings by the academic legal community, both Aboriginal
and non-Aboriginal. A comprehensive discussion of how we are to live together should include a concern for how Aboriginal citizens/nations relate to
the political arenas of Canadian federalism, to elections and legislatures, and
for their capacity to influence public policies that affect Aboriginal peoples
as such and as Canadians (Milen 1991, for a helpful survey up to 1991). The
overwhelming tendency to ignore or downplay this area presumably reflects
the natural focus of anti-colonial Aboriginal nationalism on exit by self-
government, rather than on participation in the federal and provincial political
life from which Aboriginal peoples were so long excluded. However, the limited jurisdiction of self-governing First Nation communities, the large
off-reserve population, plus the obvious importance of federal and provincial
laws and policies for all Canadians, Aboriginal or otherwise, suggest that isolation from the federal, provincial, and territorial political process would be
unfortunate for First Nations.

It is occasionally argued that there is some logical or political or constitutional incompatibility between self-government and simultaneous
participation in territorial, provincial or federal politics. In one version, the

argument is that membership/citizenship in a First Nation is incompatible with membership in the Canadian nation (See Taiaiake Alfred, quoted in Williams 2004, 93). Kiera Ladner quotes a prominent Anishnaabe scholar: "I don't vote in elections in France. I don't vote in elections in Ethiopia. Why would I vote in Canada? They are all foreign nations" (Ladner 2003*b*, 24). If this argument enjoyed universal Aboriginal support, the result would simply be to punish small communities by isolating them from their Canadian counterparts, while simultaneously providing disincentives for the governments of Canadian federalism to be concerned about their fate (Cairns 2003*b*, 8). Occasionally, the rationale for non-participation is a version of the Trudeau argument that if Quebec acquired a vast increase in jurisdiction possessed by no other province, Members of Parliament (MPs) from Quebec would have to opt out of discussion in Parliament of law and policy that applied only to Canada outside Quebec. Kymlicka applies this argument to Aboriginal MPs elected from Aboriginal districts "voting on legislation from which Aboriginals would be exempt" (Kymlicka 1995, 143).[99] However, the applicability of the Trudeau thesis to First Nations is minimal. It makes no sense to suggest that the limited legislative powers of small communities of a few hundred or a few thousand people should require the legislators who represent them to opt out of federal (provincial or territorial) legislative discussions because of marginal infringements of federal, provincial or territorial jurisdictions. In any event, no one has explained how a representative should behave when, as will typically be the case, the First Nations in his/her Aboriginal constituency possesses different jurisdictions. Curiously, no one argues that provincial legislators elected from Montreal, Toronto or Vancouver, whose law-making powers vastly exceed any jurisdiction likely to be possessed by First Nation governments, should absent themselves from policy discussions that apply to smaller communities but not to themselves. As Ovide Mercredi, subsequently Grand Chief of the Assembly of First Nations, argued in 1990: "There is no inconsistency in Canada recognizing our collective rights of self-government and us still getting involved and maintaining our involvement in the political life of the state, which means getting involved in federal elections" (cited in Schmidt 2003, 1).

Members of Aboriginal nations are, of course, free to act on their belief that to vote is to accept an unwanted citizenship in someone else's nation. Further, it is true that for many reasons Aboriginal (First Nation) electoral participation is generally low. This is both evidenced and explained in a recent issue of *Electoral Insight* (2003) devoted to "Aboriginal Participation in Elections." In Manitoba, First Nations voting turnout on reserves in federal and provincial elections declined precipitously from 65.4 percent in 1962 to 26.7 percent in 2003 (Kinnear 2003, 47). Bedford describes very significant declines in voter turnout in Nova Scotia and New Brunswick from the 1960s to the late eighties and early nineties. In New Brunswick, participation rates declined from 70 percent in the 1962 federal election to 17.8 percent in 1988, and in Nova Scotia from 89.3 percent in 1962 to 54 percent in 1988 (Bedford 2003, 17; for provincial elections across the country, see Bedford 2003, 17-20).

Bedford interprets this decline in voter participation to a weakening sense of "civic duty," to "a significant decline in the self-identification of Aboriginal persons as Canadians" in the last 40 years, and as indicating "serious and deep-seated questions about the legitimate authority of the Canadian state and its control over their lives" (ibid., 19). This voting data supports Borrows' description of Aboriginal peoples as "'uncertain citizens,' only loosely associated with the Canadian political community" (Borrows 2003, 225). The question of what is to be done is not easily answered.

Enhancing the representational role of the Assembly of First Nations and other Aboriginal organizations to speak for Aboriginal peoples in lieu of conventional politics is a high-risk enterprise given the fragility and internal tensions that are endemic features of their existence.[100] Any representational theory postulated on the two-row-wampum image of two societies travelling side-by-side down the river of life in peaceful coexistence but negligible interdependence is too removed from reality to merit serious discussion.[101] While the language of nation-to-nation relations is now commonplace, and undoubtedly reflects a post-colonial assertiveness, it is difficult to see how it could be institutionalized. It makes some sense in the treaty-making process when one First Nation is at the bargaining table with federal or provincial governments. It makes little sense, however, to assert that hundreds of individual First Nations could separately seek to successfully influence the federal, provincial, and territorial policies that are outside their jurisdiction. Even if the process of consolidation recommended by RCAP were to occur and reduce the number of nations to between 60 and 80, the processes of executive federalism could not accommodate a five-to seven-fold increase in the number of official participants. In any event, First Nations, with their small populations, lack the knowledge and bureaucratic capacity to interact successfully in executive federalism. Abele and Prince suggest that Nunavut, with 2,700 public servants and a population of 30,000, "is probably very near the lower practical limit for effective participation in executive federalism" (Abele and Prince 2003, 155). The Royal Commission on Aboriginal Peoples' nation-to-nation proposal that Aboriginal nations should have a third House in Ottawa, complementing the Senate and House of Commons, primarily acting as a check or watchdog when their behaviour threatens Aboriginal concerns, would isolate Aboriginal peoples from the mainstream politics that so decisively affects their lives.

Further, the nation-to-nation image subtly leads to a view of Canada as an international system and deflects our attention away from the reality that Aboriginal nations are part of the Canadian nation.[102] It thus deflects our attention from the vast realm of policy and legislation emanating from the governments of Canadian federalism and away from the question of how Aboriginal voices can influence that policy and legislation.[103] Federal and provincial and territorial governments have the constitutional authority to speak to and for Aboriginal members of their civic community with respect to the legislative jurisdictions they wield. How can this be made legitimate, and lose the appearance of a colonial left-over?

In a major advocacy report on the reform of Canada's electoral system, the Law Commission of Canada, responding to what it described as "a democratic malaise," (2004, xiii) and sensitive to the criticisms that the existing first-past-the-post electoral system contributed to the "under-representation of women, minority groups, and Aboriginal peoples," (ibid., xv) advocated a mixed-member proportional electoral system for Canada.[104] Under such a system, "two-thirds of the members of the House of Commons should be elected in constituency races using the first-past-the-post method, and the remaining one-third should be elected from provincial or territorial party lists," with the voter having two votes, one for a constituency representative and one for a party list (ibid., 175).

The decisiveness of the report foundered on the issue of Aboriginal representation. Although it advocated a battery of common measures to enhance the representation of women, minority groups, and Aboriginal peoples in the House of Commons, its policy proposals for representing Aboriginal peoples were incomplete or tentative. It recommended that "the federal government, in consultation with First Nations, Métis, and Inuit peoples, should explore the possibility of introducing Aboriginal Electoral Districts, as recommended by the Royal Commission on Electoral Reform and Party Financing, or a 'House of Aboriginal Peoples,' consistent with the recommendations of the Royal Commission on Aboriginal Peoples" (ibid., 178).

I have already argued that the Royal Commission proposal is seriously flawed. It would isolate First Nations from mainstream Canadian politics, and reduce their input to a largely watchdog role. The 1991 report of the Royal Commission on Electoral Reform and Party Financing did not consider proportional representation as a vehicle for overcoming the under-representation of women, ethnic minorities, and Aboriginal peoples. For the latter, it advocated guaranteed Aboriginal Electoral Districts (AEDs). The commission anticipated that up to eight AEDs could emerge. Aboriginal individuals could decide whether to be put on the Aboriginal roll, or remain as voters in individual constituencies. The number of AEDs would be determined by the numbers who opted for the Aboriginal roll (the size of AED and constituency electorates would be roughly similar). This proposal would guarantee Aboriginal representation and would allow constant comparisons of the efficacy of the two systems of representation in generating favourable results from an Aboriginal perspective (Royal Commission on Electoral Reform 1991, 169-93). On the other hand, it might distance Aboriginals from the conventional parties if the maximum number of AEDs were created, and it might decrease the sensitivity of non-Aboriginal MPs to Aboriginal concerns, as arguably occurred in New Zealand under the former system of guaranteed Maori seats (Gibbins 1991, 172).[105] Gibbins further speculates that public support for AEDs would be limited by a political culture committed to "the neutral ballot and to the use of the same ballot by all voters regardless of their income, religion, gender or race" (ibid., 183; see also 179).[106] Further, the category "Aboriginal" is an omnibus category which might result in internecine battles in

Aboriginal Electoral Districts, with candidates from larger communities carrying the day. Gibbins underlines the tensions of AEDs containing "quite disparate Aboriginal interests" identified with Indian, Inuit, and Métis (ibid., 164). Finally, in the absence of a constitutional amendment to allow AEDs to transcend provincial boundaries, there would be no AEDs in Atlantic Canada (Royal Commission on Electoral Reform 1991, 176 and 178). Accordingly, while the AED proposal is preferable to RCAP's House of Aboriginal Peoples, it is inferior to the mixed member proportional (MMP) system.

The appropriate electoral system to encourage the participation of Aboriginal peoples in electoral politics at federal, provincial, and territorial levels should satisfy two criteria: first, it should increase the number of Aboriginal representatives, and second, it should do so in a way that contributes to integrative tendencies in the party system, which means Aboriginal and non-Aboriginal representatives frequently acting together. These two criteria are linked to what Borrows calls the "fundamental question ... whether nations can develop inter-cultural norms that allow for deep diversity, while at the same time creating societies that have certain shared horizons and civic engagement" (Borrows 2003, 249; see also 251).

According to Arsenau, if the objective is the representation of non-territorial groups, "based on international experience, ... PR [proportional representation] party-list systems produce the most representative legislatures, single-member plurality first-past-the-post (FPTP) the least representative, and mixed systems something in between" (Arsenau 1999, 133).[107] The move to a pure party-list system in Canada would probably be indigestible. A long history of direct links between constituents and elected representatives has institutionalized a preference that must be respected in any electoral reform proposals. The New Zealand experience is instructive. That country moved from a Canadian-style system supplemented by four guaranteed Maori seats, to a MMP system, this time with five Maori seats. In the first election (1996) under the new system, with each voter having two votes — one for constituency representation and one for the party list — a record number of Maori MPs were elected. Maori candidates did exceptionally well on the party-list ballot, electing 9 of 55 members, and would almost certainly have done even better under a straight PR system. Under the list component of the election, Maori actually elected more than their share of the New Zealand population: 16.4 percent of the party-list seats and about 12 percent of the New Zealand population (ibid., 142; Nagel 1999, 161). Donley Studlar poses the relevant question for Canada in an article "Will Canada seriously Consider Electoral System Reform? Women and Aboriginals Should" (Studlar 1999).

In light of the New Zealand experience, the fact that Canada is one of the few countries using the first-past-the-post electoral system and given the under-representation of Aboriginal citizens by the FPTP system, and the fact that electoral reform is more prominently on the Canadian agenda than it has been for decades, a mixed member proportional system would add to the legitimacy of the constitutional order.[108] It would meet the criteria for electoral reform previously mentioned. It would increase Aboriginal representation in the House of Commons, and it would support integrative tendencies in the party system by facilitating collaboration between Aboriginal and non-Aboriginal representatives.

Canada, of course, has a Senate as well as a House of Commons at the federal level. While the primary justification for the second chamber has always been to represent the federal principle, the representation of interests and communities under-represented in the House of Commons is recurrently identified as an additional second chamber rationale. Senate defenders repeatedly refer to this role, and in the recent literature cite women and Aboriginal peoples as beneficiaries of an appointment process more able than the House of Commons electoral process to respond to the diversities of a remarkably heterogeneous society. Authors consistently note the much greater recent Aboriginal representation in the Senate (at 5 percent) compared to their House of Commons representation, or to their percentage of the Canadian population (Smith 2003, 57 and 81; see also the numerous positive references from various contributors in Joyal 2003).[109] Senator Serge Joyal, referring to Aboriginal peoples and other under-represented groups, spoke of the Senate "fulfilling its constitutional role of protecting minority and human rights ... [and of its obligation] to speak for those who would otherwise remain unheard in a majoritarian political culture" (Joyal 2003, 287).

This Senate function of enhancing the presence of Aboriginal peoples in the legislative process is a valuable corrective to the deficiencies of Aboriginal representation in the House of Commons. Even if a MMP system were to be introduced, the special constitutional status of Aboriginal peoples provides support for the degree of Senate over-representation that now exists. Aboriginal Senate representation is a composite response to Taylor I and II, in that it singles out the specificities of the Aboriginal presence in Canada but does so in a legislative chamber also responsive to the Canadian dimension.

A similar analysis can be applied to the Crown. David Smith recently noted that "it is Aboriginal people today in Canada who speak most often and with the greatest feeling about the place of the Crown in their lives" (Smith 1999, 16).[110] This attachment to the Crown is reinforced by diversifying the selection of monarchical representatives to include Aboriginal people. While no Aboriginal person has been appointed as Governor-General, three Aboriginal persons have been appointed as Lieutenant-Governors, in Alberta, Manitoba, and Ontario.

In a brilliant article published over 20 years ago, Raymond Breton documented the state-led transformation of the Canadian symbolic order (Breton 1984). The symbolic order differs from the material order in that it is not seen through the lens of an *économisme*. The symbolic order is manifest "in the multiplicity of symbols surrounding the rituals of public life, the functioning of institutions, and the public celebration of events, groups and individuals" (ibid., 125). Historically, Aboriginal peoples, especially Indian peoples (now First Nations), experienced a "constitutional stigmatization" that defined them as constitutional outsiders, lacking the relevant attributes to be admitted into the majority society (Cairns 1999*b*, 17-20 and 31-35). Their appointment as Senators and as Lieutenant Governors, the efforts to increase their numbers in legislatures, the suggestion that a Council of Elders provide advice to the Supreme Court when it considers Aboriginal issues are positive attempts to reverse yesterday's stigmatization. As Breton argues, "individuals expect to recognize themselves in public institutions. They expect some consistency between their private identities and the symbolic contents upheld by public authorities, embedded in the societal institutions, and celebrated in public events. Otherwise, individuals feel like social strangers; they feel that the society is not *their* society" (Breton 1984, 125). While it would be ludicrous to suggest that the symbolism of positive recognition can redress the multiple ills that afflict so many Aboriginal communities and individuals, it would be a misunderstanding of how societies function to always preface "symbolic" with "merely." Symbolic resources are real resources, and they can be used to pursue material, political, and other goals.

Yesterday's symbolic order profoundly disadvantaged and discriminated against Aboriginal peoples. Wise management of the symbolic order should be directed simultaneously to recognizing the special place of Aboriginal peoples in Canadian society, and to their visible inclusion in the major institutions of the Canadian constitutional order. To do so is to respond to the separate directives that flow from the analyses that inform both Taylor I and Taylor II.

Summary of Recommendations

The generation of a balance between Taylor I and Taylor II — between the desires of First Nations for recognition of their nationhood in self-government arrangements and the desire of the federal government to include Aboriginal people as Canadian citizens — leads to the following recommendations:

First, the inclusion of section 25 in the Charter is a reasonable attempt to balance the nation-building role of the Charter with the rights of indigenous nations within Canada.

Second, the Supreme Court adjudication of the Charter needs to be sensitive to Aboriginal concerns. The Charter, qualified by section 25, with a Supreme Court whose role and membership are influenced by the Charlottetown proposals, would be a reasonable balance between Taylor I and II.

Third, supporters of First Nations need to find ways to enhance their governing capacities. This should include major attention to the practicalities of self-government: skilled administrators, a profound understanding of how the federal system, of which they are a part, functions, and attempts to compensate for the limitations of small populations by collaboration with nearby First Nations. In the absence of positive changes of the above nature, the achievement of self-government will be, in too many cases, a hollow victory. Russell's observation that "few Aboriginal communities are currently prepared to implement any form of self-government" (Russell 2000, 210) may be an exaggeration, but it is made by a First Nations lawyer who describes Aboriginal self-government as "a People's Dream."

Fourth, section 35 is not doing the job of constitutional affirmation that appears to have been its clear intent. Judicial interpretation of its meaning should be less restrictive and more generous, interpreting it as an instrument of self-determination within Canada.

Fifth, given the limitations on governing capacity that will attend even the most favourable circumstances for small populations, mostly of village size, participation in the policy-making arenas at all levels of the federal system is a necessity if Aboriginal voices are to be heard. At the federal level the electoral system most likely to enhance Aboriginal representation in legislatures and encourage integrative tendencies in the party system is the mixed member proportional system.

Sixth, the Senate is an appropriate supplementary vehicle for strengthening Aboriginal representation in Parliament.

Seventh, yesterday's symbolic order, in Breton's phrase, stigmatized Aboriginal peoples. Its successor should recognize the special place of Aboriginal peoples in Canadian society by their visible presence in the major institutions of the Canadian constitutional order.

The preceding recommendations are driven by three imperatives:

One, Aboriginal peoples, nations, and individuals are part of the pan-Canadian civic community in one of their dimensions. As David Miller cogently observed, without a shared identity, Canadians "are being asked to extend equal respect and treatment to groups with whom they have nothing in common beyond the fact of cohabitation in the same political society" (cited in Schouls 2003, 82; see also Chambers 2004, 220).

Miller's position is implicitly supported by poll data that indicates divided opinion over land claims and treaty rights. A 2003 poll indicated 42 percent support for doing "away with Aboriginal Treaty rights and treat[ing] Aboriginal people the same as other Canadians." In the Prairies, 54 percent (62 percent in Saskatchewan) support doing away with Aboriginal treaty rights. Andrew Parkin, the former co-director of the Centre for Research and Information on Canada, interprets the polling data as indicating that "Canadians say that they value Aboriginal culture and want Aboriginal communities to prosper, but are uncomfortable with arrangements that suggest that Aboriginal people might be treated differently than other Canadians" (Centre for Research and Information on Canada 2003, 2).

Two, the inescapable limitations that attend self-government for small populations, most of whom as presently constituted have less than 500 people, necessarily mean that the politics and administration of the external governments of Canadian federalism are hugely important for Aboriginal peoples. They need, therefore, to so position themselves that they can systematically and predictably make their voices heard in the standard political arenas of Canadian federalism.

Three, Charles Taylor's arguments for deep-diversity recognition of Aboriginal nations (Taylor I) and his separate Taylor II argument of the necessity for democratic states to be able to mobilize their populations as citizens in the pursuit of public goals need to be integrated into a hybrid vision of the polity which seeks to accommodate Taylor I and II. This accommodation comes with a price tag, the relinquishing of goals that make reconciliation unattainable. The Canadian state has to recognize the limits to its tendency to push toward homogeneity in its citizen body. Deep diversity Aboriginal peoples need to accept, and respond to, the reality that they are "nations within," as well as the reality of their existence as nations.

Conclusion

It is tempting to think that there is a clear recipe for resolving the tensions between indigenous peoples and the states in which they live, but the temptation too often leads to disappointment. The temptation to conjure up a rosy Aboriginal future following the *Constitution Act, 1982* with its section 35 recognition clause and the section 25 exemption of Aboriginal rights and freedoms from the Charter's application is less easily held now than it was 20 years ago. Constitutional clauses, no matter how powerful their symbolism, cannot do the job alone (Borrows 2003, 247). They are, admittedly, a resource, but they can be employed by actors with other purposes than the original intent of their creators.

Borrows criticizes over-reliance on the constitution as the vehicle for reform, and notes that sections 25 and 35 have been huge disappointments in terms of Aboriginal nation-building. They "have become focused on a few specific practices that the courts decide were integral to Aboriginal peoples prior to European arrival in North America, that have not already been extinguished." Perversely, section 35 has been transformed into justification for infringing Aboriginal rights (ibid.).

Behind this failure to deliver apparently promised goods is the ambivalence of Canadians about the flourishing of Aboriginal nations pursuing separate cultural goals. Although Borrows continues to see section 35 as a lever to generate Canadian support for Aboriginal rights, the fundamental task is the education of Canadian civic society in a multitude of arenas, from kitchens and churches to cabinets and legislatures (ibid., 248-49).

Brad Morse, a leading scholar of Aboriginal affairs, makes the analogous point with respect to self-government, that disproportionate energy has focused on the question of entitlement, at the expense of attention to "the practical realities involved in making self-government work" (Morse 1999*a*, 42; see also Abele and Prince 2003, 159-60 for similar comments). Dan Russell, also writing about self-government, concurs about the danger of discussions too removed from grass-roots realities by what he describes as "academic reasoning [in the RCAP report] ... almost devoid of any practical insights" (Russell 2000, xii).

Borrows, Morse, and Russell are repeating for the Aboriginal policy area the lessons that activists and scholars learned after the failure to update the constitution by judicial review and formal amendment in the Depression of the 1930s. After World War II, the governments of Canadian federalism retreated to working the constitution with various instruments of flexibility (Smiley 1970). More recently, the bruising results of the attempts to accommodate Quebec nationalism by constitutional change have generated an aversion to seeing the constitution as a site for problem-solving (Cairns 1997*a*). The retreat from "big-bang" theories of constitutional change, or big-bang hopes for supportive judicial interpretations of clauses such as section 35 should not be misconstrued. Macro-thinking is essential if we are to have any sense of direction. Section 35 may at the moment be a sleeping giant, but it is a constitutional sleeping giant, and it may be awakened in the future when times are propitious.

The likelihood of a comprehensive implementation of the policy thrust of this postscript being implemented is minimal. The support of too many differently positioned actors with their own visions and their own analysis would be necessary. Nevertheless, I continue to believe that in deciding what to do, thinking of a blend of Taylor I and Taylor II helps to keep us on track. It positions us intellectually by providing a sense of direction. Taylor I reminds us that we must respond positively to Aboriginal nationalism. Nationalism is one of the most powerful *isms*. When its supporters combine passion and numbers, nationalism can destroy empires and shatter states. It can be accommodated, but it cannot be eliminated.

Taylor II reminds us that the nation-state monopolizes political control of the globe. Indigenous nations have to adapt to the bureaucratic nature of the modern state if they wish to work with it and influence its behaviour (Nadasdy 2003). Further, the nation-state has its own criteria of belonging, most notably citizenship, which are capable of bending but will not disappear. To say that the Canadian state seeks to embrace within a single, possibly variegated civic identity all who are subject to its policies, is to say no more than that is what states are and do.

NOTES

1.　See the following for the complexities of the historian's role in the court room: Bourgeois (1986); Dickinson and Gidney (1987); Fisher (1992); Fortune (1993).
2.　This is already a reality. See, for example, Newhouse and Peters (2003). Five of the 20 authors in this volume on "Urban Aboriginal Peoples" are urban geographers or sociologists. There are no contributions from the academic law community. Five of the ten contributors to *Aboriginal Conditions: Research as a Foundation for Public Policy* are sociologists, and one is a social demographer.

The remaining four do not identify their disciplinary background. See White, Maxim and Beavon (2003).

3. See, however, the recent essay by Loxley and Wien (2003).

4. A view strongly expressed by Monture-Angus, who writes: "I do not believe that our ideas can ever transcend our gender or our culture," and "I cannot understand male roles and responsibilities because I have not lived that particular experience," and "members of the mainstream [can never] fully understand Aboriginal culture as they can never live the life of an Aboriginal person" (Monture-Angus 1995, 4, 87 and 100). Merton's "The Perspectives of Insiders and Outsiders" is the classic analysis of the rival claims of these two categories of access to knowledge and understanding. His common sense conclusion, which I share, is that the perspectives of Insiders ("members of specified groups and collectivities or occupants of specified social statuses"), and Outsiders (who "are the non-members") complement each other (Merton 1973, 113 and 136).

5. For example, Frances Abele, a senior staff member on the Royal Commission on Aboriginal Peoples (RCAP), and a well-known scholar of Aboriginal affairs, noted the hegemony of law in the commission's thinking (Abele 1999, 17-18). This deflected attention from concerns relating to issues of workability, viability and a degree of civic solidarity with non-Aboriginal societies — concerns that are much more natural to a political scientist. See Cairns (2000a, ch. 4) for a discussion of the RCAP from a political science perspective.

6. John Borrows says it well: "we cannot ... ignore the world we live in ... In reconstructing our world we cannot just do what we want" (Borrows 1994, 23).

7. In a recent review of an edited collection on Aboriginal and treaty rights, Peter Russell tellingly congratulated Emma LaRocque for her "intellectual courage" in writing an article critical of healing circles for their lenient sentencing of rape cases. He goes on to congratulate the editor for "including LaRocque's essay," two indicators of the political pressures on Aboriginal scholars (Russell 1997, 299). See Cairns (1997a) for the impediments to discussion of, among other things, Aboriginal policy.

8. One final observation: I freely recognize that the following pages reflect a possibly old-fashioned political science that its critics might say privileges the traditional view of states in Eurocentric discourse and the international state system in which they exist. This bias, if such it may be called, possibly reflects an intellectual conservatism overly respectful of the historical globalization of the state form and insufficiently appreciative of a post-colonial political science engaged in the deconstruction of traditional concepts such as boundaries, sovereignty, etc. Although I believe I have captured a future reality when I structure the paper around the premise that indigenous aspirations have to come to terms with a Canadian state which will continue to be the dominant political formation on the northern half of North America for the foreseeable future, I may be wrong. For a helpful and provocative analysis of a post-colonial perspective that does not inform this paper, see Bruyneel (2002a). "At base," according to Bruyneel, "post-colonial political science addresses the question of the politics of sovereignty by critiquing and re-imagining how political space is and can be defined" (ibid., 3). See also Bruyneel (2002b, 28-35), section headed "Canada is the Problem: Sovereignty is the Solution," for a discussion of a non-accommodationist approach.

9. There is, of course, a third stage, the break-up of the Soviet Union and the Soviet empire, but that is outside my terms of reference.

10. However, the worldwide indigenous population is not small. Niezen estimates 300 million (Niezen 2000, 120), while Tennant (1994, 21) cites Valerie Parker's reporting of "500 million indigenous people."

11. Up until the 1960s in Canada, assimilation was the prevailing paradigm among non-Aboriginal policymakers. In 1939, at a seminar on Indian policy co-hosted by the University of Toronto and Yale University, the general impression was the inevitability of assimilation. "In the end," according to Charles Loram of Yale University, "the civilization of the white man must prevail" (Loram and McIlwraith 1943, 7-8). Thirty years later, the federal government's 1969 White Paper repeated the assumption that, to the astonishment of its authors, was repudiated by organized Indian resistance (Canada 1969).

12. Thornton observes that "men do not allocate a secondary and subordinate place to other men without developing a contempt for them. They can justify their dominance only on the assumption that these others are not worthy to share it. The subsequent anti-colonialist campaigns have accordingly had as their principal objective the release of whole peoples from this contempt, which is the most searing of all forms of bondage" (Thornton 1965, 158).

13. "If progress is accepted as desirable, and if indigenous peoples are located at the far bottom end of the ladder of progress, then it is an act of compassion and humanity to develop and assimilate indigenous peoples into modern society. Indeed, this was the self-evident and enthusiastic project of the International Labour Organization ... in the 1940s, 1950s, and 1960s: to help indigenous peoples develop out of their miserable lives and into the modern world" (Tennant 1994, 10).

14. This explains Frances Abele's observation of "a remarkable convergence with respect to fundamental goals and even political strategy" of indigenous peoples in Canada, Australia, New Zealand, Norway, and Greenland (Abele 2001, 140).

15. Barsh asserts that "developments in the international arena have begun to have an effect on indigenous people's political movements at the national level. United Nations activities have not only added to the strength of conviction of national movements, but are beginning to open up opportunities for concrete aid" (Barsh 1994, 86). Stamatopoulou states that "A major benefit that indigenous peoples draw from their participation at the UN Working Group and, of course, at the major indigenous conferences, is the strength that accompanies the awareness of common problems, common struggles, and international solidarity. Indigenous leaders whose communities are impoverished, marginalised, and often persecuted find a supportive audience at the international level and are strengthened by common goals and strategies" (1994, 69).

16. Thus, Philpott argues that "international agreement upon sovereign statehood was the terms on which a crisis of pluralism (triggered by colonial independence movements) was settled" (Cited in Bruyneel 2002*a*, 7).

17. The capacity to displace the imperial power, take control of a sovereign state, and acquire membership in the international state system does not, of course, guarantee a successful post-independence record. The colonial power often left behind state boundaries with little meaning and a population with limited identification with the new state. See Davidson (1991 and 1992) for a discussion of tropical African kleptocracies that brutalize, rob, and exploit their own people. Davidson, in fact, blames the nation-state, an ill-suited imposition on African societies, as the cause of these failings. See also Jackson (1990) for a discussion of "quasi-states" that have attained independence and international recognition,

but have limited capacity to provide leadership and services to those they ostensibly govern.

18. This is even true of the Kahnawake Mohawks described by Gerald Alfred as having "a strongly asserted radical form of nationalism ... a form of nationalist ideology which at its core rejects Canada and turns inwards toward the traditional ideal" (1995, 184). He asserts that there "is no special allegiance to Canada in Kahnawake" (ibid., 101). Nevertheless, he notes that Mohawks recognize "that certain jurisdictions require a sharing of authority with other governments" (ibid., 147), that there are "limits to autonomy imposed by a dearth of resources," and are clear that ongoing funding from Ottawa is essential. Such funding is viewed by "most Mohawks" as "reparations for previous wrongs committed against the Mohawk people" (ibid., 95, see also 99).

19. A longer version of this paper would have discussed a fourth reality — the emergence of the "Aboriginal peoples of Canada" in section 35 of the *Constitution Act, 1982,* defined as including Indians, Inuit, and Métis. The emergence of the new constitutional category "Aboriginal peoples" complicates policy-making, and generates competition among the three groups for the ear of Ottawa.

20. Newhouse agrees with Andersen. Urban Aboriginal residents "are developing a culture that is in some ways distinctly urban while at the same time distinctly Aboriginal" (Newhouse 2003, 244).

21. See Norris and Beavon (1999) for helpful analysis and data. They note the high mobility between reserves and cities in both directions, a pattern they call "churn." The availability of reserves as "home," distinguishes legal status First Nation members from other urban Aboriginals. Norris, Cooke and Clatworthy observe that "formalized membership and residency requirements (for status Indians and for reserve life) create different push-and-pull factors that influence migration and mobility" (2003, 108). "Moving back to a reserve is an alternative that is generally available only to Registered Indians" (ibid., 108 and 126).

22. Although residential segregation is in general more pronounced in the United States than in Canada, Maxim, Keane and White cite Drost *et al.* to the effect that "the relatively higher residential concentration of Aboriginals in the core city areas of the western CMAs [census metropolitan areas] may have led to ghetto effects that exacerbate the already low degree of integration of Aboriginals" (Maxim, Keane and White 2003, 81).

23. Nevertheless, the registered urban population was still significantly behind the rest of the Canadian population.

24. Guimond attributes this ethnic mobility, non-Aboriginal to Aboriginal, to three factors. Growing numbers of children from mixed ethnocultural background increase the population with a choice of ethnic identity. Various factors, including OKA and RCAP, have "restore(d) the image and pride of Aboriginal peoples," thereby bolstering the rationale for choosing an Aboriginal identity. Finally, the perception of "benefits, real or perceived, attached to "Aboriginal identity" increases the incentives to choose an Aboriginal identity (Guimond 2003, 104). Norris, Cooke and Clatworthy also note that the "impact of the 1985 amendments to the *Indian Act* has been a large increase" in the Registered Indian population in urban areas, and a smaller increase in the on-reserve population (2003,113).

25. A recent study suggested that "in many respects, an increasing segment of urban Aboriginal populations appears to be moving, or becoming positioned for entry into positions associated with new middle classes" (Wotherspoon 2003, 161).

26. The urban route is now attracting increasing attention, particularly from the Canada West Foundation. See Hanselmann and Gibbins (2002) and the references there cited, and Hanselmann (2003). See also Newhouse and Peters (2003a). The urban route attracts different disciplines than the landed community self-government route. The prominence of the academic legal community in the latter is not duplicated in the former.

27. The most prominent exception is Stewart Clatworthy (Clatworthy 1993, 1994, 2001, 2003).

28. Siggner (2003a) provides slightly different figures for urban areas.

29. In his recent history of *Peoples and Empires*, Anthony Pagden observed that: "All Aboriginal peoples are inescapably peoples of two worlds. They are Micmac and Canadian, Maori and New Zealander. They share two cultures ... No one resists the idea that cultures are porous and subject to periodic reinvention so fiercely as the spokespersons of the Aboriginal peoples. This is hardly surprising since so much of their claim depends upon an appeal to continuing cultural difference. Yet few cultures are so polymorphous as they. Everywhere in the world, they nestle within other cultures, predominantly of European origin, where they now constitute the minority" (Pagden 2001, 164-65).

30. The governance problems of small First Nations — limited capacity, kinship ties — cropped up intermittently before the Standing Committee on Aboriginal Affairs dealing with the *First Nations Governance Act*. (See Canada. Standing Committee 2003, no. 18, January 30/03, Jim Aldridge; no. 19, February 3/03, Michael Mitchell; no. 22, February 5/03, John Graham; no. 23, February 6/03 Stephen Cornell; no. 40, February 27/03, John Whyte). A preliminary attempt to assess a "Community Capacity Index" was published as this essay was in its final stages. See Maxim and White (2003).

31. See Cairns (2000b) for a critical discussion of RCAP.

32. David Miller, although he refers specifically to "aboriginal groups such as native Americans and Australian aborigines," can be assumed to include First Nations in Canada as he puzzles over how they should be classified. They are clearly not ethnic groups, but "their social and political structure is not sufficiently developed for them to constitute integral nations rivalling the dominant national groups in the states to which they belong" (Miller 2001, 301 n. 4).

33. Technically, these figures refer to registry groups (627 in 2001) rather than bands (612 in 2001), both of which need to be distinguished from reserves (2,675 in 2001) (Canada. DIAND 2002, xv, viii).

34. Frances Abele suggests that there are, "depending on how the counting is done, between 40 and 60 First Nations" (2001, 141). Paul Chartrand suggests 35 to 50 "distinct nations, meaning peoples in the usually accepted international sense of a group with a common cultural and historical antecedence" (1999, 104).

35. In an important article, Robert White-Harvey documents the typically land-poor reality of Indian reserves in Canada in contrast to both Australia and the United States. In Canada, "officials recognized only small individual sub-divisions of larger tribes, and left these small bands dispersed across thousands of tiny and isolated reserves ... while dozens or even hundreds of bands may speak similar languages and share common cultural traditions, Ottawa still chooses to ignore the reality of the larger tribes to deal instead only with the small bands which it created under its law" (White-Harvey 1994, 590; see also 601). See also Tennant's (1990, 9), observation that the larger tribal groups [in BC] "were officially and resolutely ignored" (cited in White-Harvey 1994, 590).White-Harvey concludes: "Native

self-government will be a hollow victory if First Nations have little land and resources to govern. The present micro-sized and dispersed reserves show demonstrably little potential for ever providing a basis for economic renewal from within the Native communities, or for freedom from economic wardship" (ibid., 611).

36.   DIAND definitions are as follows: *Rural*: First Nation between 50 and 350 kilometres from the nearest service centre having year-round road access. *Remote*: First Nation over 350 kilometres from nearest service centre having year-round access. *Special access*: First Nation has no year-round access to the nearest service centre, and experiences higher transportation costs (Canada. DIAND 2003, 107).

37.   Brad Morse, University of Ottawa law professor and Aboriginal expert, observed that many First Nations are very small — "not large enough to sustain what the aspirations may be ... [in which case] many of these jurisdictions are going to be hollow, because there's just not the human resource base or the population to be able to, for example, effectively run hospitals when you have a community of 100 people." A helpful alternative, he suggested, would be to consolidate some of the smaller nations into a larger "regional government" (Morse 1999*b*, 330).

38.   See the critique by the Ojibway education consultant, Harvey McCue, of the "misguided overarching [on-reserve education] policy of ... dealing one on one with individual bands, regardless of their size, capacity or internal resources ... this approach ... is grossly inefficient, ignores economies of scale, [and] motivates mismanagement ... How can any serious observer or bureaucrat reasonably expect all 680 or so bands, the majority of them with fewer than 1,000 residents and situated in rural and remote locations, to manage effectively an education program with limited and inexperienced internal resources in the absence of anything even remotely resembling" the educational infrastructures and resources available in the provinces (McCue 2001, 18).

39.   For a nuanced discussion by a leading anthropologist of the previous generation of "the directions, the scope and the net result of cultural change in the small and comparatively powerless communities associated with Indian reserves," see Hawthorn (1971, 63). He concluded in 1971 that "it is ... clear that change is continuous and far-reaching and has directions that can be ascertained. Although there may not be an end-point for the existence of many small communities, the sum of the adaptations has so far increased the similarity of all of them to the national community" (ibid., 81).

40.   See the provocative discussion of "capital reserves" by White-Harvey, "a large tract of land to be used for the economic and social benefit of a group of related First Nations" (1994, 607-10). See also the discussion of urban reserves by Loxley and Wien (2003, 225-26) and the more elaborate discussion in Barron and Garcea (1999).

41.   See, for example, Wilkins (2000, 250 n. 24), beginning "As a non-Aboriginal person..."

42.   See Tully (1999) for an elaboration.

43.   See Weaver (1981) for a general discussion.

44.   "Fit" is less of a problem in the urban setting where nation is less available as a solidary unit.

45.   "Not surprisingly," wrote Hawthorn in 1971, "many Indians have no doubts that they are now worse off and continue to regret what they regard as their losses" (Hawthorn 1971, 67).

46.   A few years ago, Rick Ponting observed that the foremost theme in Indian discourse is "the 'untrustworthiness of government.' The federal government ...

was repeatedly portrayed as betraying trust, being deceitful, lying, not dealing in good faith, and being insincere or hypocritical" (Ponting 1990, 93). Cree leader Billy Diamond reported that his father taught him "one thing ... never, never agree with the government — no matter what, and I never have. Never" (MacGregor 1989, 4).

47. Since 1986, many First Nation communities have refused to participate in the census for a variety of reasons (e.g., expression of their sovereignty, distrust of government). Incompletely enumerated reserves often make trends, over different census years, more difficult to interpret because it is not always the same reserves that are participating from census to census (Norris and Beavon 1999, 9).

48. See also Canada (1996, vol. 2(1) 4, 243 and 374-75) for additional observations on the illegitimacy of Canadian governments and political institutions.

49. Three of the four Aboriginal commissioners in the seven-member commission played leading roles in Aboriginal associations. Viola Marie Robinson was president of the Native Council of Canada from 1990–91. Mary Sillet had been vice-president of the Inuit Tapirisat Canada for four years and president of the Inuit Women's Association of Canada for two terms. Georges Erasmus, commission co-chair, was National Chief of the Assembly of First Nations from 1985–91. This background of leading roles in Aboriginal associations did not, of course, dictate a negative assessment of traditional, representative democracy, but it undoubtedly tilted evaluation in that direction. According to William Johnson, Erasmus, who joined the Company of Young Canadians in the 1960s and studied Frantz Fanon's *The Wretched of the Earth*, told Johnson in 1975 that it was "my bible" (Johnson 2002).

50. In his concluding remarks, however, Mercredi observed that "we can and do participate in the political life of our country" (Mercredi 1990, 5). See Knight (2001) for a helpful analysis of Aboriginal ambivalence toward guaranteed parliamentary representation, which he favours, and toward Parliament itself.

51. According to Roger Gibbins, if "electoral participation [to select members of parliament is] ... a measure of health for the political community ... in the case of Canada's Aboriginal peoples, the vital signs are often distressingly weak" (Gibbins, quoted in Knight 2001, 1068).

52. According to Tony Hall, the refusal of a number of prairie First Nations to allow polling stations on their reserves for the Charlottetown Accord, reflected "a strong current of opinion ... that ... participating in the vote ... would be inconsistent with the distinct constitutional status of Indian societies in Canada" (Hall 1992, 1).

53. Bedford and Pobihuschy conclude that: "By their participation rates in Canadian elections Aboriginal people appear to be telling us that they have little confidence in the likelihood of finding a comfortable domicile within the Canadian state" (Bedford and Pobihuschy 1994, 35). Kiera Ladner argues that voting turnout is "on average, considerably lower than among the general Canadian public." The Canadian political system is not seen as an instrument of liberation, but of "their domination and oppression." For treaty peoples, "voting in Canadian elections entails both participating in an alien system and engaging in an act (interfering with the business of another nation) their nation promised it would never do" (Ladner 2003*b*, 21, 23 and 25).

54. The Chief Electoral Officer noted that because an elector could vote even if his/her name was not on the official list by swearing an oath, votes cast as a percentage of electors on the list "should, therefore, be used only as a rough guide to voter turnout" (Chief Electoral Officer, Nunavut 1999, 28).

55.   The Chief Electoral Officer reported that because an elector could vote even if his/her name was not on the official list by swearing an oath, "total votes cast as percentage of electors on the list should, therefore, be used only as a rough guide to voter turnout" (Chief Electoral Officer, Northwest Territories 2000, 1).

56.   According to Floyd McCormick, Deputy Clerk, Yukon Legislative Assembly, "First Nations people are an increasingly important political constituency, as voters and candidates," including such high-profile candidates as the former head of the Council for Yukon Indians, Eric Fairclough, First Nations, who briefly led the territorial NDP following the 2000 election (McCormick 2002). In 1987, following a by-election victory, five of the nine NDP members of a majority government (16 seats in all) were First Nation MLAs (ibid.).

57.   Twenty-one percent of Yukon's population in 1996 was Aboriginal (up from 14 percent in 1971); 48 percent of the Northwest Territories population was Aboriginal in that year, 85 percent of Nunavut's population was Aboriginal, and 75 percent of the Aboriginal population was Inuit (Canada. DIAND 2003, 75).

58.   See Brock (2002) for an excellent discussion, and Jamieson (2002) for a critical First Nations perspective. Nault delegitimates the AFN by referring to it as a "lobby group," which Matthew Coon Come vehemently denies with the assertion that "we are part of the institutions of Canada ... mentioned ... in the Constitution [which] gives us a special place" (Barnsley 2002*e*, 3). Nault refers to the "leadership and the organization ... as dysfunctional" because of an inability to work with the federal government (Barnsley 2002*d*, 3). Coon Come counters by likening Nault to "a 19th century cotton-plantation union-buster" (Barnsley 2002*c*, 8; see also Barnsley 2002*a*, 2003*a*, 3 and 9 for more on the controversy between Nault and Coon Come). Internal AFN difficulties are highlighted by an editorial in the *Windspeaker*, "All This Time and This is the Answer?" which asserts that "if the AFN doesn't get its act together there may not be an organization to lead in the next three years" (*Windspeaker*, December 2002, 4). Nault repeated his claim that the AFN was dysfunctional the following year (Barnsley 2003*b*, 11-12). In the same issue of *Windspeaker*, an editorial "Sour Grapes: Lots of Wrath," underlined the profound tension in the AFN between sovereigntists and supporters of integration, including the National Chief, Phil Fontaine *(Windspeaker* 2003; see also Simpson 2003 on tensions within the AFN over the best strategy to deal with Ottawa). Coon Come admits that the AFN is "an umbrella organization with a national chief who is, to a significant extent, a figurehead" (Coon Come 2001). Early in his tenure Coon Come proposed that the National Chief should be directly elected by First Nation members, thus taking the power away from the chiefs, a proposal coolly received by the chiefs (Hunter 2001; see Gray 2002 for a positive assessment of Coon Come). The tension between Matthew Coon Come and the federal government was also played out at the Durban "World Conference Against Racism, Racial Discrimination, Xenophobia and Related Intolerance," August/September 2001. Coon Come compared the Canadian "racist and colonial syndrome of dispossession and discrimination" with South African apartheid. Jean Chrétien reprimanded Coon Come, and Robert Nault, INAC minister, stated that if there was no apology, Coon Come would "find it very difficult for people to do business with him" (Cooper 2004, 243; see also Gray 2002). At the 1993 Vienna conference, relations between Canadian diplomats and indigenous leaders were estranged, partly because indigenous demands were seen as threatening Canadian sovereignty, and the fear that concessions to indigenous representatives would

complicate the struggle with Quebec independentistes (Cooper 2004, 126 and 142).

59. "The *Constitution Act, 1982*, has dramatically changed the relationship between all Aboriginal groups and the rest of Canada....The effect of these provisions has had a profound impact upon the jurisprudence as well as upon the political stature and public profile of the Aboriginal peoples in Canada" (Morse 2002*a*, 73).

60. For example, Nault admits that the First Nations *Governance Act* is an example of section 91(24) thinking, which Coon Come critiques as a hierarchical paternalistic anachronism, in contrast to section 35 of the constitution which legitimates a nation-to-nation relationship (Barnsley 2002*a*, 3). Hurley notes that one basis of AFN opposition to the First Nations *Governance Act* was the fact that it was "based on subsection 91(24) of the 1867 Constitution rather than a rights-based approach under section 35 of the *Constitution Act, 1982*" (Hurley 2002, 37-38). The tension between these two visions surfaced in the evidence presented to the Standing Committee on Aboriginal Affairs (2003) to consider the First Nations *Governance Act*. (See Canada. Standing Committee 2003, no. 15, January 28/03, Matthew Coon Come; no. 20, February 4/03, Wendy Cornet; no. 39, February 26/03, Anna Hunter.)

61. See Brad Morse (2002*b*) for a devastating critique of the *Indian Act*, especially sections 1–3 and 36–38. Hurley notes that the *Indian Act's* fundamental flaws are well-known, including its paternalism, its archaic nature, and its assimilative purpose. However, it has "provided certain protections. These conflicting roles together with differing views of federal authorities and First Nations on the nature and scope of the inherent right of Aboriginal self-government under section 35 of the *Constitution Act, 1982*, have intensified the complexities of reforming the *Indian Act*" (Hurley 2002, 2).

62. The following studies reveal a range of distrust and suspicion of provincial governments. Crossley (1995), re: PEI; Milne (1995) re: New Brunswick; Aucoin (1995) and Paul (2000) re: Nove Scotia; Cameron and Wherrett (1995) re: Ontario; Brock (1995) re: Manitoba; Rasmussen (1995) re: Saskatchewan; Mitchell and Tennant (1994) re: BC; Kaufman and Roberge (2000, 15 and 30) re: the three prairie provinces; Alfred (1995, 17-18) re: Kahnawake Mohawks and Quebec; Goodleaf (1995), Ciaccia (2000) and York and Pindera (1991) re: the Oka crisis and Quebec-Mohawk relations. See, also the critique of the BC referendum process and results by Paul Barnsley. (Barnsley 2002*a*, ch. 6). Bob Rae, as premier of Ontario, and committed to improving First Nation conditions, encountered "a deep strain of tradition that the relation between settlers and natives is a relationship between the Crown and first peoples [summarized in the view that]: 'settler governments' at the provincial level are deeply suspect in this view, and should just get out of the way" (Rae 1996, 167). At the time of the Quebec referendum (1995) two First Nations, Cree and Montagnais as well as Inuit, held their own referendums, and overwhelmingly supported the position that if Quebec were to secede they would remain with Canada. Inuit voted 95 percent "no," Cree 96 percent "no," and the French-speaking Montagnais 99 percent "no" (Cairns 1996, 36; see also Wherrett 1996).

63. The RCAP report presents ample reasons why Canadian citizenship is not warmly embraced (Canada 1996, vol.1). The "uncertain citizen" status noted by Borrows was reinforced by the geographical fragmentation of Indian peoples into small communities which limited the likelihood of electing one of their own to the House of Commons.

64. Writing in 1985, Boldt and Long assert that "Indians do not see themselves as fully participating Canadian citizens and have shown little interest in such participation. They do not participate meaningfully in the legislative or bureaucratic aspects of any level of government other than their own tribal governments. The Canadian government does not derive and never has derived its power to govern Indians from the consent of Indian people" (Boldt and Long 1985, 177). See also, among others, Carens (2000, ch. 8); Johnston (1993); the edited collection by Kymlicka and Norman (2000); and Boldt (1993, 50, 73-4, 83 and 108).

65. "Enfranchisement," in the powerful language of Darlene Johnston of the Chippewas of Nawash band, "involved ... rejection of the values that community membership represented. It meant standing outside the circle that contained one's ancestors, language, traditions, and spirituality" (Johnston 1993, 362; see also Foster 1999, 361).

66. See Carens (2000, 188-93) for a nuanced discussion of the Charter and Aboriginal governance. Wilkins provides a judicious and comprehensive footnoted survey of the issue of whether the Charter does or should apply to First Nation governments (Wilkins 1999).

67. See Mercredi and Turpel (1993, 96-106); Boldt and Long (1985, 171, quoting the AFN).

68. See McNeill for the thesis that "as a matter of Canadian constitutional law, with the exception of the section 28 gender equality provisions, the *charter* does not apply to Aboriginal governments" (1996, 61). He also argues that the "consent [of Aboriginal peoples] should be a prerequisite to the application of the *charter* to their governments" (ibid., 70).

69. Although Alfred disagrees: "Native peoples do not take the present internal-colonial system as their reference point ... most Native peoples view non-Native institutions as transitory and superfluous features of their political existence" (Alfred 1995, 7).

70. For example, although Trevor Knight reports that "many Aboriginal people argue that ... guaranteed Aboriginal representation ... is not a goal worth achieving" (Knight 2001, 1092), it is clear from his lengthy analysis that Aboriginal opinion is divided on the issue.

71. This is also true of Taylor's famous essay "The Politics of Recognition" (Taylor 1992).

72. This is close to Bernard Crick's position: "The practices of a common citizenship hold together real differences of national, religious and ethnic identities to the mutual advantage of minorities and majorities alike" (Crick 2000, 136).

73. As Banting (1999) observes, the developing relation between the welfare state and societies that are multicultural, multinational, or both is intellectually contested territory. His sweeping survey does not include the very small Aboriginal nations in Canada. He pleads for more research.

74. "It is ... important," Taylor states, "that societies based on the legitimating idea of popular sovereignty have to be able to understand themselves as deciding together, and therefore deliberating together, and this presupposes a certain common focus, a common sense of what the society is concerned with, around which public debate takes its shape. In the absence of this, no common debate is possible at all. But if no common debate, then no common decision. And if no common decision, then the very legitimacy of the polity is in question, because this stems from the idea that the established order has been willed by every-

one ... This means that refusal of diversity may not be animated solely by narrowness and ill will ... It may also come from a genuine and not entirely fanciful fear. Which is why the proposal to build a more open, equal, diverse, mutually enriching society has to meet these fears with believable proposals for a new political identity" (Taylor 2001, 4).

75.   A brilliant survey of the Burnt Church conflict by Ian Stewart documented the tension and violence between non-Aboriginal fishermen and the MicMac over the *Marshall* decision. The former are unsympathetic to any "special ascriptive [MicMac] right" to fish, which MicMac view as an inherent pre-existing right confirmed, but not based on treaties in 1760–61. Stewart concludes that "Canada may be a rights-conscious society, but rights that are universalistic, rather than particularistic, are much more likely to generate widespread enthusiasm" (Stewart 2002, 354 and 361).

76.   See also Henderson (1994*a, b*) and Henderson, Benson and Findlay (2000) for treaty federalism.

77.   Tully suggests that a "shared history," albeit differently understood, is a "special bond that holds the partners, and indeed the country, together in an intercultural dialogue" (Tully 1999, 428).

78.   See Borrows (1999, 78-79) for a contrary interpretation of the Gus Wen Tah, the two-row-wampum, which stresses sharing, mutuality, interdependence, and interconnectedness.

79.   In a recent review, Peter Russell referred "to a missing ingredient in the normative vision of many reformers in this field — the common principles and institutions which Aboriginal and non-Aboriginal Canadians must share if their post-colonial relationship is to be based on a shared citizenship in a single, though deeply federal, overarching Canadian political community. A relationship built solely on respect for difference meets only one of the two ideals expressed in the two-row-wampum belt; it satisfies the separateness aspect, but not the interconnectedness aspect. The two canoes, Aboriginal and non-Aboriginal, are fated to share the same river. Giving that river a shape and substance that is truly post-colonial is as important as ensuring that one of the canoes no longer threatens to swamp the other" (Russell 1997, 299).

80.   For example, see the statement by Robert Nault that First Nations must be "part of our constitutional family, and in our constitutional family the senior government is the federal government" (Barnsley 2003*b*, 11-12).

81.   Even "an autonomous Aboriginal nation would encounter a geography, history, economics, and politics that requires participation with Canada and the world to secure its objectives" (Borrows 1999, 74-75).

82.   Taylor not only repeatedly stresses the necessity of "sharing identity space," arguing that "there is no alternative," but underlines the impediments to successfully doing so. Democracies, he notes, which need cohesion, have "a strong temptation to exclude those who cannot or will not fit easily into the identity with which the majority feels comfortable, or believes alone can hold them together" (1999, 279-80, 286; see also 265, 274 and 277).

83.   In "Tales of Constitutional Origin and Crown Sovereignty in New Zealand," P.G. McHugh documents the crisis of "constitutionalism in the postcolonial age" in New Zealand, and the necessary task of putting the New Zealand Constitution on a new principled basis capable of incorporating the Maori presence and the Treaty of Waitangi. The constitutional past has to be reconstituted to

"incorporate elements more responsive to a present state of affairs," he argues. "It must reinvent itself or perish with the order it can no longer justify" (McHugh 2002, 71-72).

84. This is a goal more easily stated than reached. Brad Morse, writing in 2002, stated: "It has only been over the past three decades that as a society we have moved away from the policies of complete assimilation that was [sic] championed in the federal White Paper of 1969. This has not been an easy transformation in the thinking and attitudes of non-Aboriginal peoples, nor has this change been accepted by all. This change has, however, been made far more difficult for federal and provincial governments that have vigorously resisted the development of a new relationship based upon mutual respect and the sharing of the bounty of this land" (Morse 2002*b*, 93).

85. See also Ratner, Carroll and Woolford (2003) for the complexities, misunderstandings, and dissimilar life-worlds that pervade the BC treaty-making process.

86. See the theme issue of *Citizenship Studies* (2003) on indigenous peoples/state relationships.

87. This was recently recommended for Canada by Archbishop Desmond Tutu, with a focus on residential schools. (See Wiwa 2001; Valpy 2001; and *The Globe and Mail* 2001). Graham Fraser (2001) also offers general support. Bhikhu Parekh underlines the difficulty of redress and reconciliation: "As a rule, perpetrators of injustice do not want to remember the past and their victims do not wish to forget it, and their divided attitudes to it render a shared future impossible. It is vital to avoid both obsessive brooding over the past and a willed amnesia and to confront, understand and accept the past as well as break with it by rectifying its injustices and agreeing to conduct future relations on a just basis" (Parekh 2000, 212).

88. Taylor sympathetically cites Parekh, whose book he is reviewing, "that justice is not the only end that we seek in our social life, and we need to balance its requirements against those of 'social harmony, integration of the excluded groups into mainstream society, a rich and vibrant cultural life, and a sense of social solidarity'" (Taylor 2001, 4).

89. This appears to be very close to Michael Ignatieff's position: "We've got to find a way to do justice by Aboriginal peoples and simultaneously maintain the unity of Canadian citizenship that depends on equal rights for all, but also to reconcile competing ideas of fairness — it is fair given that [the Aboriginals] were the first inhabitants of this country for them to have special claims. And if we believe in the rule of law, we have to take our treaty obligations very seriously. The [Massey] lectures are trying to say that we've got two visions of citizenship, and the very idea of the country, and they've both got to be true" (Richler 2000, 4).

90. See Cairns (2001) for a discussion of the complexities of a constitutionalized multinational Canada.

91. In his recent book *Hunters and Bureaucrats*, Paul Nadasdy provides the specifics for McDonnell and Depew's observation. He brilliantly documents the irresistible pressures on the Kluane people living in a "relatively small and out-of-the-way corner of the world" (2003, 56) in the Yukon to "implicitly restructure their societies by developing their own bureaucratic infrastructures modelled on and linked to those of the governments with which they must deal" in negotiating land claims and co-management agreements. Indeed, the "new relationship between First Nations peoples and the state [which these agreements involve]

simply would not be possible without the bureaucratization of First Nations societies." The result is that First Nations peoples are "also agreeing to abide by a whole set of implicit assumptions about the world, some of which are deeply antithetical to their own." Such is the price paid to make "relations between First Nations, Canada, and the provinces/territories possible" (Nadasdy 2003, 2-7).

92.   As McDonnell and Depew point out: "Aboriginal people today are just that; they are contemporaries who, quite apart from being the proud inheritors of distinct traditions ... may have developed sensibilities with regard to gender equality, individual rights, and a host of other values that may be contrary or contradictory to [past] tradition" (McDonnell and Depew 1999, 369).

93.   Schouls' observation is apposite: "it is generally argued that, if Aboriginal self-governing communities are to retain their ties with Canada, they must accept certain commitments to shared citizenship, among them the Charter. The cost of Canadian citizenship to Aboriginal peoples, in other words, is the requirement that Aboriginal governments forgo those cultural practices that violate basic Charter rights" (Schouls 2003, 100-01). See, however, the section 25 qualification to the Charter's application to Aboriginal peoples.

94.   This proposal is congruent with Borrows' thesis that "it is ... incumbent upon Canadian judges to draw upon Indigenous legal sources more often and more explicitly in deciding Aboriginal issues" (Borrows 2002*a*, 5; see also 2002*b*). These sources, of course, will involve oral tradition, discussed in Borrows (2002*c*, 86-92), a focus that unites the chapters in Borrows, *Recovering Canada.* "My central purpose in this book is to demonstrate that Aboriginal law continues to exist as an important source of legal authority in Canada, even if it has been weakened through the unjust imposition of alien structures" (ibid., 88).

The role of elders is complicated by the fact that their "questioning [by] ... lawyers and judges [is] inconsistent with their status in their communities [and] ... for Elders from certain groups ... such treatment is tantamount to discrediting their reputation and standing in the community" (ibid., 91).

95.   Schouls' observation is relevant: "Aboriginal communities that regularly average 1,000 members or fewer are simply incapable, by virtue of small populations and limited resources, of building communities independent from the Canadian mainstream. Aboriginal communities are in constant discussions with Canadian governments, ranging from treaty negotiations to social service delivery agreements, transfers of monies, and investment in reserve-based capital expenditures. Clearly, Aboriginal communities remain reliant on the non-Aboriginal majority for resources critical to community development. Promoting cultural strategies that isolate Aboriginal communities from their Canadian counterparts ... may well jeopardize the relations of interdependence that now serve as the life blood for Aboriginal communal existence" (Schouls 2003, 83). See also Schouls for the limited options for "relatively small Aboriginal communities" (2003, 140).

96.   Although RCAP structured its massive report around the concept of nation, and the nation-to-nation relationship, it went on to "disqualif[y] small communities and bands [from nation status] because they do not possess the necessary institutional sophistication or resources to make the running of modern complex governmental organizations viable" (Schouls 2003, 77).

97.   The 2004 progress report of the BC Treaty Commission, which discusses the 44 negotiation tables now underway, indicates a number of consolidations that have occurred for treaty-making purposes (BC Treaty Commission 2004, 19.3).

98. For the Métis, according to Mark Stevenson, "the constitutional promises held out by s.35 ... have been all but illusionary" (Stevenson 2003, 65; see also 96-98).

99. Clearly, at some level of enhanced Quebec jurisdiction, the argument could emerge that the rationale for electoral participation by the Quebec population in Canadian affairs had completely disappeared.

100. The *Windspeaker* has frequent accounts of these difficulties. For a recent example, see Barnsley (2004).

101. In his plea for greater use of indigenous law in Canadian courts, Borrows asserts that: "A legal doctrine focused exclusively upon the differences between Aboriginal and non-Aboriginal people would distort the reality both of Crown-Aboriginal relations and Aboriginal peoples' lives. Aboriginal and non-Aboriginal people have developed ways of relating to one another which, over the centuries, have produced numerous similarities between the various groups. Moreover, Aboriginal and non-Aboriginal people often share interests in the same territories, ecosystems, economies, ideologies, and institutions. While imperfect, and often skewed to the disadvantage of Aboriginal people, these points of connection cannot be ignored" (Borrows 2002*a*, 9-10).

 Elsewhere, Borrows argues that the two-row-wampum, in addition to asserting the autonomy of the British and First Nations, also contains "a counterbalancing message that signifies the importance of sharing and interdependence [that makes it] ... clear that ideas of citizenship must also be rooted in notions of mutuality and interconnectedness" (Borrows 2002*d*, 149).

102. This, of course, is strenuously contested by supporters of treaty federalism, which is passionately argued and supported by Kiera Ladner (Ladner 2003).

103. Gibbins correctly observes that even for the best endowed Aboriginal governments and their citizens, "the federal and provincial governments will continue to legislate in areas having a substantive impact on Aboriginal communities — environmental policy, post-secondary education, health care and so forth" (Gibbins 1991, 181).

104. To the commission, "it has become apparent that the first-past-the-post electoral system no longer meets the democratic aspirations of many Canadians" (Law Commission of Canada 2004, 15; see also, Law Commission of Canada 2002).

105. Fleras agrees that the "major weakness [of separate Maori seats in New Zealand was that it made] both Maori and non-Maori representatives ... accountable only to the particular community that elected them ... [which] isolates the Maori agenda by encouraging non-Maori MPs to pigeon-hole Maori concerns away from the political centre" (Fleras 1991, 95-96).

106. In New Zealand, prior to the recent introduction of the MMP system, there was "widespread *Pakeha* antipathy to [separate] Maori seats" (Fleras 1991, 75).

107. Although reserve-based First Nations obviously have a territorial base, their small populations deprive them of winning seats proportionate to their votes under first-past-the-post electoral systems.

108. Arsenau correctly notes that effective representation will not automatically follow from proportional representation of the New Zealand variety. "Political parties, even under PR, have to be committed to recruiting women and Aboriginal candidates, to placing these candidates high on the party-list and, once elected, to giving these MPs access to cabinet posts" (Arsenau 1999, 144).

 Nagel reports considerable electorate disillusionment in New Zealand following the first MMP election, partly due to inflated hopes when it was introduced, linked to the overselling of its virtues. The public was surprised and frustrated to find that (i) "proportionality of seats does not entail proportionality of power." (ii) "Empowerment of previously disadvantaged groups can lead to growing pains in the body politic." (iii) "Coalition government does not mean consensus government" (Nagel 1999, 158).

109. At the time of the November 2000 election, Aboriginal representation at 6.1 percent of Senate membership was nearly four times greater than the 1.6 percent Aboriginal membership in the House of Commons (Joyal 2003, Appendix 326).

110. "Aboriginal Canadians least of all Canadians desire an end to the Crown," observed David Smith, "while more than most they endow it with political substance" (Smith 1999, 231).

REFERENCES

Abele, Frances (1999), "The People's Commission." Paper presented to the annual meeting of the Canadian Political Science Association, Université de Sherbrooke, 6 June.

—— (2001), "Small Nations and Democracy's Prospects," *Inroads* 10.

Abele, Frances and Michael J. Prince (2003), "Aboriginal Governance and Canadian Federalism: A To-Do List for Canada," in François Rocher and Miriam Smith, eds., *New Trends in Canadian Federalism* (Peterborough: Broadview Press).

Alfred, Gerald R. (1995), *Heeding the Voices of our Ancestors: Kahnawake Mohawk Politics and the Rise of Native Nationalism* (Toronto: Oxford University Press).

Alfred, Taiaiake (1999), *Peace, Power, Righteousness: An Indigenous Manifesto* (Toronto: Oxford University Press).

Andersen, Chris (2002), "Courting Colonialism: Contemporary Métis Communities and the Canadian Judicial Imagination." Paper presented at "Reconfiguring Aboriginal-State Relations," conference, Queen's University, 1-2 November.

Arsenau, Therese (1999), "Electing Representative Legislatures: Lessons from New Zealand," in Henry Milner, ed., *Making Every Vote Count: Reassessing Canada's Electoral System* (Peterborough: Broadview Press).

Aucoin, Peter (1995), "Canadian Governments and Aboriginal Peoples Project, Province of Nova Scotia." RCAP Project on Canadian Governments and Aboriginal Peoples (unpublished paper).

Augustine, Roger J. and Guy A. Richard (2002), *Miramichi Bay Community Relations Panel, Building Bridges: Miramichi Fishing Communities at a Crossroad.* Available at www.dfo-mpo.gc.ca/COMMUNIC/Marshall/miramichi-rep_e.htm.

Banting, Keith (1999), "Social Citizenship and the Multicultural Welfare State," in Alan C. Cairns *et al.*, eds., *Citizenship, Diversity, and Pluralism: Canadian and Comparative Perspectives* (Montreal and Kingston: McGill-Queen's University Press).

Barnsley, Paul (2002a), "Police Powers Worry Critics," *Windspeaker* 20 (3).

—— (2002b), "Does the New Language Mean a New Approach?" *Windspeaker* 20 (4).

—— (2002c), "National Chief Comes off the Ropes Swinging," *Windspeaker* 20 (4).

—— (2002d), "Feds to Abandon 30 Negotiation Tables," *Windspeaker* 20 (6).

—— (2002e), "Chief, Minister Spar over Throne Speech," *Windspeaker* 20 (7).

Barnsley, Paul (2003a), "Minister Accused of Abuse of Power," *Windspeaker* 20 (9).

—— (2003b), "Governance Act Dead, for now – Nault," *Windspeaker* 21 (8).

—— (2004), "Assembly of Chiefs? Hooky Playing Chiefs Disrupt Annual Meeting," *Windspeaker* (September).

Barron, F. Laurie and Joseph Garcea, eds. (1999), *Urban Indian Reserves: Forging the New Relationship in Saskatchewan* (Saskatoon: Purich Publishing).

Barsh, Russel Lawrence (1994), "Indigenous Peoples in the 1990s: From Object to Subject of International Law," *Harvard Human Rights Journal* 7.

Bauch, Hubert (2002), "Charter Turns 20," *Montreal Gazette*, 13 April.

BC Treaty Commission (2002a), *"Annual Report 2001*, including "Looking Back, Looking Forward: A Review of the BC Treaty Process" (Vancouver: The Commission).

—— (2002b), *Self-Government Matters: Harvard Study.* Update, May.

—— (2004), *Consider: Annual Report* (Vancouver: The Commission).

Beavon, Daniel and Martin Cooke (1998), "Measuring the Well-Being of First Nation Peoples" (unpublished paper).

—— (2003), "An Application of the United Nations Human Development Index to Registered Indians in Canada, 1996," in Jerry P. White, Paul S. Maxim and Dan Beavon, eds., *Aboriginal Conditions: Research as a Foundation for Public Policy* (Vancouver: UBC Press).

Bedford, David (2003), "Aboriginal Voter Participation in Nova Scotia and New Brunswick," *Electoral Insight* 5 (3).

Bedford, David and Sidney Pobihuschy (1994), "Aboriginal Voter Participation." Paper presented at the annual meeting of the Canadian Political Science Association, University of Calgary, 12 June.

Boldt, M. (1993), *Surviving as Indians: The Challenge of Self-Government* (Toronto: University of Toronto Press).

Boldt, M. and J.A. Long (1985), "Tribal Philosophies and the Canadian Charter of Rights and Freedoms," in M. Boldt and J.A. Long, eds., *The Quest for Justice: Aboriginal Peoples and Aboriginal Rights* (Toronto: University of Toronto Press).

Borrows, John (1994), "Contemporary Traditional Equality: The Effect of the Charter on First Nation Politics," *University of New Brunswick Law Journal* 43.

—— (1999), "'Landed' Citizenship: Narratives of Aboriginal Political Participation," in Alan C. Cairns *et al.*, eds., *Citizenship, Diversity, and Pluralism: Canadian and Comparative Perspectives* (Montreal and Kingston: McGill-Queen's University Press).

—— (2001), "Uncertain Citizens: Aboriginal Peoples and the Supreme Court," *Canadian Bar Review* 80.

—— (2002a), "With You or Without You: First Nations Law in Canada," in John Borrows, *Recovering Canada: The Resurgence of Indigenous Law* (Toronto: University of Toronto Press).

—— (2002b), "Frozen Rights in Canada: Constitutional Interpretation and the Trickster," in John Borrows, *Recovering Canada: The Resurgence of Indigenous Law* (Toronto: University of Toronto Press).

—— (2002c), "Nanabush Goes West: Title, Treaties, and the Trickster in British Columbia," in John Borrows, *Recovering Canada: The Resurgence of Indigenous Law* (Toronto: University of Toronto Press).

—— (2002d), "Landed' Citizenship: An Indigenous Declaration of Independence," in John Borrows, *Recovering Canada: The Resurgence of Indigenous Law* (Toronto: University of Toronto Press).

—— (2003), "Measuring A Work in Progress: Canada, Constitutionalism, Citizenship and Aboriginal Peoples," in Ardeth Walkem and Halie Bruce, eds., *Box of Treasures or Empty Box? Twenty Years of Section 35* (Penticton, BC: Theytus Books).

Bourgeois, Donald J. (1986), "The Role of the Historian in the Litigation Process," *Canadian Historical Review* 67 (2).

Breton, Raymond (1984), "The Production and Allocation of Symbolic Resources: An Analysis of the Linguistic and Ethnocultural Fields in Canada," *The Canadian Review of Sociology and Anthropology* 21 (2).

Brock, Kathy L., (1995), "Relations with Canadian Domestic Governments: Manitoba." RCAP Project on Canadian Governments and Aboriginal Peoples (unpublished paper).

—— (2002), "First Nations, Citizenship and Democratic Reform." Paper prepared for the UBC Press Festschrift in Honour of Alan Cairns.

Bruyneel, Kevin (2002a), "A Pitch for a Postcolonial Political Science." Paper prepared for presentation at the annual meeting of the American Political Science Association, Boston, 29 August–1 September.

—— (2002b), "Smash your Protractor! The Complicated Geometry of Aboriginal Politics in Canada." Paper prepared for presentation at the annual meeting of the Canadian Political Science Association, Toronto, 31 May.

Bull, Hedley (1984), "*The Revolt Against the West,*" in Hedley Bull and Adam Watson, eds., *The Expansion of International Society* (Oxford: Clarendon Press).

Cairns, Alan C. (1992a), *Charter versus Federalism: The Dilemmas of Constitutional Reform* (Montreal and Kingston: McGill-Queen's University Press).

—— (1992b), "Reflections on the Political Purposes of the Charter: The First Decade," in Gerald A. Beaudoin, ed., *The Charter: Ten Years Later* (Cowansville, Quebec: Les Editions Yvon Blais Inc.).

—— (1996), "The Legacy of the Referendum: Who Are We Now?" *Constitutional Forum* 7 (2/3).

—— (1997a), "Why Is it so Difficult to Talk to Each Other?" *McGill Law Journal* 42(1).

—— (1997b), *Constitutional Reform: The God that Failed.* Transactions of the Royal Society of Canada. Volume VII, *Can Canada Survive? Under What Terms and Conditions?* ed. David M. Hayne (Toronto: University of Toronto Press).

—— (1999a), "Introduction," in Alan C. Cairns *et al.*, eds., *Citizenship, Diversity, and Pluralism: Canadian and Comparative Perspectives* (Montreal and Kingston: McGill-Queen's University Press).

—— (1999b), "Constitutional Stigmatization," in Patrick J. Hanafin and Melissa S. Williams, eds., *Identity, Rights and Constitutional Transformation* (Aldershot: Ashgate Publishing).

—— (2000a), *Citizens Plus: Aboriginal Peoples and the Canadian State* (Vancouver: University of British Columbia Press).

—— (2000b), "Report of the Royal Commission on Aboriginal Peoples: Aboriginal Nationalism, Canadian Federalism and Canadian Democracy" (unpublished paper).

—— (2000c), "The End of Internal Empire: The Emerging Aboriginal Policy Agenda," in David M. Hayne, ed., *Governance in the 21ˢᵗ Century.* Transactions of the Royal Society of Canada, Volume X (Toronto: University of Toronto Press).

—— (2001), "Searching for Multinational Canada: The Rhetoric of Confusion," *Review of Constitutional Studies* 6 (1).

Cairns, Alan C. (2003*a*). "Afterword: International Dimensions of the Citizen Issue for Indigenous Peoples/Nations," *Citizenship Studies* 7 (4).

——— (2003*b*) "Aboriginal People's Electoral Participation in the Canadian Community," *Electoral Insight* 5 (3).

Cameron, David and Jill Wherrett (1995), *New Relationships, New Challenges: Aboriginal Peoples and the Province of Ontario.* RCAP project on Canadian Governments and Aboriginal Peoples, Final Report (unpublished paper).

Canada (1969), *Statement of the Government of Canada on Indian Policy.* Presented to the First Session of the Twenty-eighth Parliament by the Honourable Jean Chrétien, Minister of Indian Affairs and Northern Development (Ottawa: Department of Indian Affairs and Northern Development).

——— (1987), *Senate Debates,* 18 November.

——— (1996), *Report of the Royal Commission on Aboriginal Peoples* , 5 vols. (Ottawa: Canadian Communication Group Publishing).

Canada. Department of Indian Affairs and Northern Development (DIAND) (2002), *Registered Indian Population by Sex and Residence 2001* (Ottawa: First Nations and Northern Statistics Section, DIAND).

——— (2003), *Basic Departmental Data, 2002* (Ottawa: First Nations and Northern Statistics Section, DIAND).

Canada. Minister of Indian Affairs and Northern Development (2002), *Bill C-61.* An Act Respecting Leadership Selection, Administration and Accountability of Indian Bands, and to Make Related Amendments to Other Acts. First Reading, 14 June 2002 (Ottawa: House of Commons of Canada).

Canada. Standing Committee on Aboriginal Affairs, Northern Development and Natural Resources (2003), re *First Nations Governance Act* (Ottawa: Government of Canada).

Carens, Joseph H. (2000), *Culture, Citizenship, and Community: A Contextual Explanation of Justice as Evenhandedness* (Oxford: Oxford University Press).

Centre for Research and Information on Canada (2003), *Canadians Want Strong Aboriginal Cultures But are Divided on Aboriginal Rights* (Ottawa: Centre for Research and Information on Canada).

Chambers, Simone (2004), "Representing Pluralism: A Comment on Pyrcz, Warren, and Kernerman," in David Laycock, ed., *Representation and Democratic Theory* (Vancouver: UBC Press).

Chartrand, Paul (1999), "Aboriginal Peoples in Canada: Aspirations for Distributive Justice as Distinct Peoples: An Interview with Paul Chartrand," in Paul Havemann, ed., *Indigenous Peoples' Rights in Australia, Canada, and New Zealand* (Auckland: Oxford University Press).

Chase, Steven (2001), "Ottawa Plans to Resume Consultations on Indian Act," *The Globe and Mail,* 29 August.

Chief Electoral Officer, Nunavut (1999), *Election of the First Legislative Assembly of Nunavut, 1999: Official Voting Results* (Yellowknife: Chief Electoral Officer).

Chief Electoral Officer, Northwest Territories (2000), *Election of the Fourteenth Legislative Assembly of the Northwest Territories, Official Voting Results* (Yellowknife: Chief Electoral Officer).

Chief Electoral Officer, Yukon (2000), *The Report of the Chief Electoral Officer of the Yukon on the 2000 General Election* (Yukon: Chief Electoral Officer).

——— (2003), *The Report of the Chief Electoral Officer of the Yukon on the 2002 General Election* (Yukon: Chief Electoral Officer).

Ciaccia, John (2000), *The Oka Crisis: A Mirror of the Soul* (Dorval, PQ: Maren Publications).

Citizenship Studies (2003), Special Issue: "Aboriginal Citizenship," 7 (4).

Clatworthy, Stewart J. (1993), *Population Implications of the 1985 Amendments to the Indian Act* (Ottawa: Assembly of First Nations).

—— (1994), *Revised Projection Scenario Concerning the Population Implications of Section 6 of the Indian Act* (Winnipeg: Four Directions Consulting Group).

—— (2001), *First Nations Membership and Registered Indian Status* (Ottawa: Indian and Northern Affairs Canada).

—— (2003), "Impacts of the 1985 Amendments to the Indian Act on First Nations Populations," in White, Maxim and Beavon, eds., *Aboriginal Conditions*.

Conquest, Robert (2000), *Reflections on a Ravaged Century* (New York: Norton).

Coon Come, Matthew (2001), "We Have a Dream, Too," *The Globe and Mail*, 31 January.

Cooper, Andrew F. (2004), *Tests of Global Governance: Canadian Diplomacy and United Nations World Conferences* (Tokyo, New York, Paris: United Nations University Press).

Cornell, Stephen (2000), Evidence (presented to the) Standing Committee on Aboriginal Affairs and Northern Development, 6 June.

Cornell, Stephen and Joseph P. Kalt, eds. (1992) *What Can Tribes Do? Strategies and Institutions in American Indian Economic Development* (Los Angeles: American Indian Studies Center, University of California).

Cornell, Stephen, Miriam Jorgensen and Joseph P. Kalt (2002), "The First Nations Governance Act: Implications of Research Findings from the United States and Canada: A Report to the Office of the British Columbia Regional Vice-Chief, Assembly of First Nations" (Tucson, AZ: Udall Center for Studies in Public Policy, University of Arizona, unpublished paper).

Crick, Bernard (2000), *Essays on Citizenship* (London and New York: Continuum).

Crosbie, John C. (2003), "Letter to the Editor," *National Post*, 18 January.

Crossley, John (1995), "Relations between the Province and Aboriginal Peoples in Prince Edward Island." RCAP Project on Canadian Governments and Aboriginal Peoples (unpublished paper).

Davidson, Basil (1991), "Dying Africa," *London Review of Books*, 11 July.

—— (1992), *The Black Man's Burden: Africa and the Curse of the Nation-State* (New York: Times Books).

Deloria, Vine (1970), *We Talk You Listen: New Tribes, New Turf* (New York: Macmillan).

Dickinson, G.M. and R.D. Gidney (1987), "History and Advocacy: Some Reflections on the Historian's Role in Litigation," *Canadian Historical Review* 68 (4).

Dyck, Noel (1991), *What is the Indian Problem?* (St. John's, Nfld.: Institute of Social and Economic Research).

—— (1995), "Telling It Like It Is! Some Dilemmas of Fourth World Ethnography and Advocacy," in Noel Dyck and James B. Waldram, eds., *Anthropology, Public Policy and Native Peoples in Canada* (Montreal and Kingston: McGill-Queen's University Press).

Electoral Insight (2003), "Aboriginal Participation in Elections," 5 (3).

First Nations Circle on the Constitution (1992), *To the Source: Commissioners' Report* (Ottawa: Assembly of First Nations).

Fisher, Robin (1992), "Judging History: Reflections on the Reasons for Judgment in *Delgamuukw v. BC*," *BC Studies* 95 (Autumn).

Flanagan, Tom (2001), "Unmasking the Warrior Chiefs," *National Post*, 25 July.

Fleras, A. (1991), *"Aboriginal Electoral Districts for Canada: Lessons from New Zealand,"* in Robert A. Milen, ed., *Aboriginal Peoples and Electoral Reform in Canada* (Toronto and Oxford: Dundurn Press).

—— (1999), "Politicising Indigeneity: Ethno-Politics in White Settler Dominions," in P. Havemann, ed., *Indigenous Peoples' Rights in Australia, Canada, and New Zealand* (Auckland: Oxford University Press).

Fleras, Augie and Roger Maaka (2000), "Reconstitutionalizing Indigeneity: Restoring the 'Sovereigns Within,'" *Canadian Review of Studies in Nationalism* 27 (1/2).

Fortune, Joel R. (1993), "Constructing Delgamuukw: Legal Arguments, Historical Argumentation, and the Philosophy of History," *University of Toronto Faculty of Law Review* 51 (1).

Foster, Hamar (1999), "Indian Administration from the Royal Proclamation of 1763 to Constitutionally Entrenched Aboriginal Rights," in Paul Havemann, ed., *Indigenous Peoples' Rights in Canada, Australia and New Zealand* (Oxford: Oxford University Press).

Four Directions Consulting Group (1997), *Implications of First Nations Demography: Final Report* (Ottawa: Department of Indian Affairs and Northern Development).

Franks, C.E.S. (2000), "Rights and Self-government for Canada's Aboriginal Peoples," in C. C. Cook and J.D. Lindau, eds., *Aboriginal Rights and Self-government: The Canadian and Mexican Experience in North American Perspective* (Montreal and Kingston: McGill-Queen's University Press).

Fraser, Graham (2001), "We Take Ease of Integration for Granted," *Toronto Star*, 9 September.

—— (2002), "Rights Document Now Part of Quebec's Fabric," *Toronto Star*, 14 April.

Gibbins, Roger (1991), "Electoral Reform and Canada's Aboriginal Population: An Assessment of Aboriginal Electoral Districts," in Robert A. Milen, ed., *Aboriginal Peoples and Electorazl Reform in Canada* (Toronto and Oxford: Dundurn Press).

The Globe and Mail (2001), "A Healing Commission for Canada's Natives," editorial. 8 May.

—— (2002), "The Haida Case," editorial. 8 March.

Goldmann, Gustave and Andrew Siggner (1995), "Statistical Concepts of Aboriginal People and Factors affecting the Counts in the Census and the Aboriginal Peoples Survey," in *Towards the XXIst Century: Emerging Socio-Demographic Trends and Policy Issues in Canada*. Proceedings of the 1995 Symposium Organized by the Federation of Canadian Demographers, St. Paul University, Ottawa, 23–25 October.

Goodleaf, Donna (1995), *Entering the War Zone: A Mohawk Perspective on Resisting Invasions* (Penticton, BC: Theytus Books).

Gray, John (2002), "The Chief's Justice," *Elm Street,* April.

Green Joyce (1993), "Constitutionalizing the Patriarchy: Aboriginal Women and Aboriginal Government," *Constitutional Forum* 4, 4.

—— (2002), "Self-Determination, Citizenship, and Federalism as Palimpsest." Paper presented to the "Reconfiguring Aboriginal-State Relations in Canada" conference, Queen's University, 1 November.

Guimond, Eric (2003), "Changing Ethnicity: The Concept of Ethnic Drifters," in White, Maxim and Beavon, eds., *Aboriginal Conditions.*

Habermas, Jurgen (2001), *The Post-National Constellation: Political Essays* (Cambridge, UK: Polity Press).

Hall, Tony (1992), "The Assembly of First Nations and the Demise of the Charlottetown Accord" (unpublished paper).

Hanselmann, Calvin (2003), "Ensuring the Urban Dream: Shared Responsibility and Effective Urban Aboriginal Voices," in Newhouse and Peters, eds., *Not Strangers in These Parts.*

Hanselmann, Calvin and Roger Gibbins (2002), "Another Voice is Needed: Intergovernmentalism in the Urban Aboriginal Context." Paper presented at the "Reconfiguring Aboriginal-State Relations in Canada" conference, Queen's University, 1-2 November.

Harris, Cole (2002), *Making Native Space: Colonialism, Resistance and Reserves in British Columbia* (Vancouver: UBC Press).

Hawkes, David C. (2002), "Rebuilding the Relationship: The 'Made in Saskatchewan' Approach to First Nations Governance." Paper presented at the "Reconfiguring Aboriginal-State Relations" conference, Queen's University, 1-2 November.

Hawthorn, H.B., ed. (1966/67), *A Survey of the Contemporary Indians of Canada,* 2 vols. (Ottawa: Queen's Printer).

—— (1971), "The Survival of Small Societies," *Anthropologica, N.S.* 13 (1/2).

Henderson, James [sakej] Youngblood (1994a), "Empowering Treaty Federalism," *Saskatchewan Law Review* 58 (2).

—— (1994b), "Implementing the Treaty Order," in Richard Gosse *et al.,* eds., *Continuing Poundmaker and Riel's Quest* (Saskatoon: Purich Publishing and College of Law, University of Saskatchewan).

Henderson, James (Sakej) Youngblood, Marjorie L. Benson and Isobel M. Findlay (2000), *Aboriginal Tenure in the Constitution of Canada* (Toronto: Carswell).

Hume, Mark (2002) "Haida Sue for Queen Charlottes," *National Post,* 6 March, pp. A1, A10.

Humphreys, Adrian (1999), "Gangsters Out to Beat the Rap," *National Post,* 21 August.

Hunter, Justine (2001),"Coon Come Faces Test at Meeting," *National Post,* 17 July.

Hurley, Mary C. (2002), *Bill C-7: The First Nations Governance Act* (Library of Parliament, Parliamentary Research Branch).

Indian and Northern Affairs Canada (2002), *Summary of the First Nations Governance Act* (Ottawa: Minister of Indian Affairs and Northern Development).

Irwin, Honourable Ronald A. (Minister of Indian Affairs and Northern Development) (1995), *Aboriginal Self-Government: The Government of Canada's Approach to Implementation of the Inherent Right and the Negotiation of Aboriginal Self-Government* (Ottawa: Minister of Indian Affairs and Northern Development).

Irwin, Robert (2001), "An Urbane Scholar in a Wilderness of Tigers," review of Abdulaziz Al-Sudairi, *A Vision of the Middle East: An Intellectual Biography of Albert Hourani,* in *London Review of Books,* 25 January.

Jackson, Robert H. (1990), *Quasi-States: Sovereignty, International Relations and the Third World* (Cambridge: Cambridge University Press).

Jamieson, Roberta (2002), "A Fresh Start on Nation-Building." Paper delivered at a Special Assembly of First Nations, Ottawa, 19 November.

Johnson, William (2002), "The Danger of Preaching Paranoia," *The Globe and Mail,* 19 December.

Johnston, Darlene (1993), "First Nations and Canadian Citizenship," in William Kaplan, ed., *Belonging: The Meaning and Future of Canadian Citizenship* (Montreal and Kingston: McGill-Queen's University Press).

Joyal, Serge ed., (2003), *Protecting Canadian Demnocracy: The Senate You Never Knew* (Montreal and Kingston: McGill-Queen's University Press).

Kaufman, Jay and Florence Roberge (2000), "The Future of Global and Regional Integration. Case Study: Aboriginal Governance in the Canadian Federal State 2015." Paper prepared for the "Future of Global and Regional Integration Project," Institute of Intergovernmental Relations, Queen's University (unpublished paper).

Kiernan, V.G. (1972), *The Lords of Human Kind: European Attitudes to the Outside World in the Imperial Age* (Harmondsworth, Middlesex: Penguin Books).

Kinnear, Michael (2003), "The Effect of the Expansion of the Franchise on Turnout," *Electoral Insight* 5 (3).

Knight, Trevor (2001), "Electoral Justice for Aboriginal Peoples in Canada," *McGill Law Journal* 46.

Kymlicka, Will (1995), *Multicultural Citizenship: A Liberal Theory of Minority Rights* (Oxford: Clarendon Press).

—— 1998. *Finding Our Way: Rethinking Ethnocultural Relations in Canada* (Toronto: Oxford University Press).

Kymlicka, Will and Wayne Norman, eds. (2000), *Citizenship in Diverse Societies* (Oxford/New York: Oxford University Press).

Ladner, Kiera L., (2003*a*), "Treaty Federalism: An Indigenous Vision of Canadian Federalism," in François Rocher and Miriam Smith, eds., *New Trends in Canadian Federalism,* 2nd edition (Peterborough: Broadview Press).

—— (2003*b*), "The Alienation of Nation: Understanding Aboriginal Electoral Participation," *Electoral Insight* 5 (3).

LaPrairie, Carol (1995), *Seen but Not Heard: Native People in the Inner City* (Ottawa: Department of Justice).

Law Commission of Canada (2002), *Renewing Democracy: Debating Electoral Reform in Canada: Discussion Paper* (Ottawa: Law Commission of Canada).

—— (2004), *Voting Counts: Electoral Reform for Canada* (Ottawa: Law Commission of Canada).

Lee, Jeff and Craig McInnes (2002), "We Can Find a Way to Live with Canada," *Vancouver Sun*, 7 March, pp. A1, A4c.

Loram, C.T. and T.F. McIlwraith, eds. (1943), *The North American Indian Today* (Toronto: University of Toronto Press).

Loxley, John and Fred Wien (2003), "Urban Aboriginal Economic Development," in Newhouse and Peters, eds., *Not Strangers in these Parts.*

Lunman, Kim (2004), "New Minister Aims to Improve the Lives of Canada's Natives," *The Globe and Mail,* 2 August.

MacGregor, Roy (1989), *Chief: The Fearless Vision of Billy Diamond* (Markham: Viking/Penguin).

Macklem, Patrick (2001), *Indigenous Difference and the Constitution of Canada* (Toronto: University of Toronto Press).

Malloy, Jonathon and Graham White (1997), "Aboriginal Participation in Canadian Legislatures," in Robert J. Fleming and J.E. Glenn, eds., *Fleming's Canadian Legislatures, 1997,* 11th edition (Toronto: University of Toronto Press).

Maxim, Paul S. and Jerry P. White (2003), "Toward an Index of Community Capacity: Predicting Community Potential for Successful Program Transfer," in Jerry P. White, Paul S. Maxim and Dan Beavon, eds., *Aboriginal Conditions: Research as a Foundation for Public Policy* (Vancouver: UBC Press).

Maxim, Paul S., Carol Keane and Jerry White (2003), "Urban Residential Patterns of Aboriginal People in Canada," in Newhouse and Peters, eds., *Not Strangers in these Parts.*

McCormick, Floyd (2002), e-mail to Cairns, 12 and 22 October.

McCue, Harvey (2001), "Indian Education Not Quite Making the Grade," *Anishinabek News* 13 (1).

McDonnell, R.F. and R.C. Depew (1999), "Aboriginal Self-Government and Self-Determination in Canada: A Critical Commentary," in John H. Hylton, ed., *Aboriginal Self-Government in Canada: Current Trends and issues,* 2nd edition (Saskatoon: Purich Publishing).

McHugh, P.G. (2002), "Tales of Constitutional Origins and Crown Sovereignty in New Zealand," *University of Toronto Law Journal* 52.

McNeil, Kent (1996), "Aboriginal Governments and the Canadian Charter of Rights and Freedoms," *Osgoode Hall Law Journal* 34 (1).

—— (2001a), "Aboriginal Governments and the Canadian Charter of Rights and Freedoms," in *Emerging Justice? Essays on Indigenous Rights in Canada and Australia* (Saskatoon: Native Law Centre, University of Saskatchewan).

—— (2001b), "The Decolonization of Canada: Moving Toward Recognition of Aboriginal Governments," in *Emerging Justice? Essays on Indigenous Rights in Canada and Australia* (Saskatoon: Native Law Centre, University of Saskatchewan).

—— (2001c), "Emerging Constitutional Space for Aboriginal Governments," in *Emerging Justice? Essays on Indigenous Rights in Canada and Australia* (Saskatoon: Native Law Centre, University of Saskatchewan).

Mendelson, Michael and Ken Battle (1999), *Aboriginal People in Canada's Labour Market* (Ottawa: Caledon Institute of Social Policy).

Mercredi, Ovide, Vice-Chief Manitoba Region Assembly of First Nations (1990), "Presentation to the Royal Commission on Electoral Reform and Party Financing," 19 April (unpublished paper).

Mercredi, Ovide and Mary Ellen Turpel (1993), *In the Rapids: Navigating the Future of First Nations* (Toronto: Penguin Books).

Merton, Robert K. (1973), "The Perspectives of Insiders and Outsiders," in Robert K. Merton, *The Sociology of Science: Theoretical and Empirical Investigations* (Chicago and London: University of Chicago Press).

Milen, Robert A. (1991), "Aboriginal Constitutional and Electoral Reform," in Robert A. Milen, ed., *Aboriginal Peoples and Electoral Reform in Canada* (Toronto and Oxford: Dundurn Press).

Miller, David (2001), "Nationality in Divided Societies," in Alain-G. Gagnon and James Tully, eds., *Multinational Democracies* (Cambridge: Cambridge University Press).

Miller, J.R. (2004), *Lethal Legacy: Current Native Controversies in Canada* (Toronto: McClelland & Stewart).

Milne, David (1995), "The Case of New Brunswick-Aboriginal Relations." RCAP Project on Canadian Governments and Aboriginal Peoples (Unpublished paper).

Mitchell, Darcy A. and Paul Tennant (1994), "Government to Government: Aboriginal Peoples and British Columbia." A Report Prepared for the Royal Commission on Aboriginal Peoples (Unpublished paper).

Monture-Angus, Patricia (1995), *Thunder in My Soul: A Mohawk Woman Speaks* (Halifax: Fernwood Publishing).

—— (1999), *Journeying Forward: Dreaming First Nations' Independence* (Halifax: Fernwood Publishing).

Morse, Bradford (n.d.) "Twenty Years of Charter Protection: The Status of Aboriginal Peoples Under the Canadian Charter of Rights and Freedoms" (unpublished paper).

Morse, Bradford (1999*a*), "Evidence Before the Standing Committee on Aboriginal Affairs and Northern Development," *Minutes of Proceedings*, 23 November.

—— (1999*b*), "The Inherent Right of Aboriginal Governance," in John H. Hylton, ed., *Aboriginal Self-Government in Canada: Current Trends and Issues*, 2nd edition (Saskatoon: Purich Publishing).

—— (2002*a*) "Comparative Assessments of the Position of Indigenous Peoples in Quebec, Canada and Abroad" (unpublished paper).

—— (2002*b*) "The Critical Imperatives for Change in the Indian Act" (unpublished paper).

Murphy, Michael (2004), "Looking Forward without Looking Back: Jean Chrétien's Legacy for Aboriginal State Relations," *Review of Constitutional Studies* 9 (1/2).

Nadasdy, Paul (2003), *Hunters and Bureaucrats: Power, Knowledge, and Aboriginal-State Relations in the Southwest Yukon* (Vancouver: UBC Press).

Nagel, Jack H. (1999), "The Defects of its Virtues: New Zealand's Experience with MMP," in Henry Milner, ed., *Making Every Vote Count: Reassessing Canada's Electoral System* (Peterborough: Broadview Press).

Native Women's Association of Canada (n.d.), *Native Women and the Charter: A Discussion Paper* (Ottawa: Native Women's Association of Canada).

Newhouse, David (2003), "The Invisible Infrastructure: Urban Aboriginal Institutions and Organizations," in Newhouse and Peters, eds., *Not Strangers in these Parts*.

Newhouse, David and Evelyn Peters, eds. (2003*a*), *Not Strangers in these Parts: Urban Aboriginal Peoples* (Ottawa: Policy Research Initiative).

—— (2003*b*), "Introduction," in Newhouse and Peters, eds., *Not Strangers in these Parts*.

Niezen, Ronald (2000), "Reconfiguring Indigenism: Canadian Unity and the International Movement of Indigenous Peoples," *Comparative Studies in Society and History* 42 (1).

Norris, Mary Jane and Daniel Beavon (1999), "Registered Indian Mobility and Migration: An Analysis of the 1996 Census Data." Paper presented at the Canadian Population Society Meeting, Lennoxville, Quebec, 9-11 June.

Norris, Mary Jane and Stewart Clatworthy (2003), "Aboriginal Mobility and Migration Within Urban Canada: Outcomes, Factors and Implications," in Newhouse and Peters, eds., *Not Strangers in these Parts*.

Norris, Mary Jane, Martin Cooke and Stewart Clatworthy (2003), "Aboriginal Mobility and Migration Patterns and the Policy Implications," in Jerry P. White, Paul S. Maxim and Dan Beavon, eds., *Aboriginal Conditions: Research as a Foundation for Public Policy* (Vancouver: UBC Press).

Pagden, Anthony (2001), *Peoples and Empires* (New York: Modern Library).

Parekh, Bhikhu (2000), *Rethinking Multiculturalism: Cultural Diversity and Political Theory* (Cambridge, MA: Harvard University Press).

Paul, Daniel N. (2000), *We Were Not the Savages: A Mi'kmaq Perspective on the Collision between European and Native American Civilizations*, New Twenty-First Century Edition (Halifax: Fernwood Publishing).

Perham, Margery (1970), *Colonial Sequence 1949 to 1969* (London: Methuen).

Ponting, J. Rick (1990), "Internationalization: Perspectives on an Emerging Direction in Aboriginal Affairs," *Canadian Ethnic Studies* 22 (3).

Rae, Bob (1996), *From Protest to Power: Personal Reflections on a Life in Politics* (Toronto: Penguin Books).

Rasmussen, Ken (1995), "The Case of Saskatchewan-Aboriginal Relations: Royal Commission on Aboriginal Peoples." Canadian Government and Aboriginal Peoples Project (unpublished paper).

Ratner, R.S., William K. Carroll and Andrew Woolford (2003), "Wealth of Nations: Aboriginal Treaty Making in the Era of Globalization," in John Torpey, ed., *Politics and the Past: On Repairing Historical Injustices* (New York/Oxford: Rowman and Littlefield).

Ray, Arthur J., with Jim Miller and Frank Tough (2000), *Bounty and Benevolence: A History of Saskatchewan Treaties* (Montreal and Kingston: McGill-Queen's University Press).

Richards, John (2004), "Creating Choices: Rethinking Aboriginal Policy" (unpublished paper).

Richards John and Aidan Vining (2003), "Educational Outcomes of Aboriginal Students in British Columbia: The Impact of 'Good Schools' on Test Scores," in Newhouse and Peters, eds., *Not Strangers in these Parts*.

—— (2004), *Aboriginal Off-Reserve Education*. C.D. Howe Institute Commentary No. 198 (Toronto: C.D. Howe Institute).

Richler, Noah (2000), "Canada Has all the Right Problems," *National Post*, 6 November.

Royal Commission on Electoral Reform and Party Financing (1991), *Reforming Electoral Democracy*, vol. 1 (Ottawa: Minister of Supply and Services Canada).

Russell, Dan (2000), *A People's Dream: Aboriginal Self-Government in Canada* (Vancouver: UBC Press).

Russell, Peter (1997), review of Michael Asch, ed., *Aboriginal and Treaty Rights in Canada: Essays on Law, Equity, and Respect for Difference* (Vancouver: UBC Press, 1997) in *Alberta Law Review* 36 (1).

Schmidt, Jennifer (2003), "Aboriginal Representation in Governmment, A Comparative Examination" (Ottawa: Law Commission of Canada, unpublished paper).

Schouls, Tim (2003), *Shifting Boundaries: Aboriginal Identity, Pluralist Theory, and the Politics of Self-Government* (Vancouver: UBC Press).

Seidle, Leslie (1996), "The Canadian Electoral System and Proposals for Reform," in A. Brian Tanguay and Alain G. Gagnon, eds., *Canadian Parties in Transition,* 2nd edition, (Scarborough: Nelson Canada Ltd).

Siggner, Andrew J. (2002), "Aboriginal Population in Canada: A Demographic Overview" (Ottawa: Statistics Canada, unpublished paper).

—— (2003*a*) "The Challenge of Measuring the Demographic and Socio-Economic Conditions of the Urban Aboriginal Population," in Newhouse and Peters, eds., *Not Strangers in These Parts*.

—— (2003*b*), "Urban Aboriginal Populations: An Update using the 2001 Census Results," in Newhouse and Peters, eds., *Not Strangers in these Parts*.

Simpson, Jeffrey (1998), "Aboriginal Conundrum," *The Globe and Mail*, 15 October.

—— (2002), "Burnt Church Report Cuts to the Chase," *The Globe and Mail*, 26 April.

—— (2003), "Good luck Mr. Fontaine: You'll need it," *The Globe and Mail*, 25 July.

Smiley, Donald V. (1970), *Constitutional Adaptation and Canadian Federalism Since 1945: Documents of the Royal Commission on Bilingualism and Biculturalism,* 4 (Ottawa: Information Canada).

Smith, David E. (1999), *The Republican Option in Canada, Past and Present* (Toronto: University of Toronto Press).

—— (2003), *The Canadian Senate in Bicameral Perspective* (Toronto: University of Toronto Press).

Stamatopoulou, Elsa (1994), "Indigenous Peoples and the United Nations: Human Rights as a Developing Dynamic," *Human Rights Quarterly* 16 (1).

Stevenson, Mark (2003), "Section 35 and Métis Aboriginal Rights: Promises Must be Kept," in Ardeth Walkem and Halie Bruce, eds., *Box of Treasures or Empty Box? Twenty Years of Section 35* (Penticton, BC: Theytus Books).

Stewart, Ian (2002), "Communities in Conflict: Nova Scotia After the *Marshall* Decision," in Hamish Telford and Harvey Lazar, eds., *Canada: The State of the Federation 2001: Canadian Political Cultures in Transition* (Montreal and Kingston: McGill-Queen's University Press).

Studlar, Donley (1999), "Will Canada Seriously Consider Electoral Reform? Women and Aboriginals Should," in Henry Milner, ed., *Making Every Vote Count: Reassessing Canada's Electoral System* (Peterborough: Broadview Press).

Taylor, Charles (1992), "The Politics of Recognition," in Charles Taylor and Amy Gutmann, eds., *Multiculturalism and the Politics of Recognition* (Princeton: Princeton University Press).

—— (1993), *Reconciling the Solitudes: Essays on Canadian Federalism and Nationalism,* Guy Laforest, editor (Montreal and Kingston: McGill-Queen's University Press).

—— (1996), "Why Democracy Needs Patriotism," in Joshua Cohen, ed., *For Love of Country: Debating the Limits of Patriotism/Martha C. Nussbaum with Respondents* (Boston: Beacon Press).

—— (1999), "Democratic Exclusion (and its Remedies?)," in Alan Cairns *et al.*, eds., *Citizenship, Diversity, and Pluralism: Canadian and Comparative Perspectives* (Montreal and Kingston: McGill-Queen's University Press).

—— (2001), "How to be Diverse: The Need for a Looser 'Us' to Accommodate 'Them'", a review of Bhikhu Parekh, *Rethinking Multiculturalism*, in *Times Literary Supplement*, 20 April.

Tennant, Chris (1994), "Indigenous Peoples, International Institutions, and the Legal Literature from 1945-1993," *Human Rights Quarterly* 16 (1).

Tennant, Paul (1990), *Aboriginal Peoples and Politics: The Indian Land Question in British Columbia, 1849/1989* (Vancouver: UBC Press).

Thornton, A.P. (1965), *The Doctrine of Imperialism* (New York: John Wiley & Sons).

Tully, James (1999), "Aboriginal Peoples Negotiating Reconciliation," in James Bickerton and Alain-G. Gagnon, eds., *Canadian Politics,* 3rd edition (Peterborough: Broadview Press).

Turpel, Mary Ellen (1989/90), "Aboriginal Peoples and the Canadian Charter: Interpretive Monopolies, Cultural Differences," *Canadian Human Rights Yearbook* 6.

—— (1992), "Indigenous Peoples' Rights of Political Participation and Self-Determination: Recent International Legal Developments and the Continuing Struggle for Recognition," *Cornell International Law Journal* 25 (3).

Valpy, Michael (2001), "S. African Model Could Help Natives Heal: Tutu," *The Globe and Mail*, 5 May.

Walkem, Ardeth (2003), "Constructing the Constitutional Box: The Supreme Court's Section 35(1) Reasoning," in Ardeth Walkem and Halie Bruce, eds., *Box of Treasures or Empty Box? Twenty Years of Section 35* (Penticton, BC: Theytus Books).

Walkem, Ardeth and Halie Bruce (2003), "Introduction," in Ardeth Walkem and Halie Bruce, eds., *Box of Treasures or Empty Box? Twenty Years of Section 35* (Penticton, BC: Theytus Books).

Weaver, Sally M. (1981), *Making Canadian Indian Policy: The Hidden Agenda 1968-1970* (Toronto: University of Toronto Press).

—— (1990), "A New Paradigm in Canadian Indian Policy for the 1990s," *Canadian Ethnic Studies* 22 (3).

Wherrett, Jill (1996), *Aboriginal Peoples and the 1995 Quebec Referendum: A Survey of the Issues* (Ottawa: Library of Parliament).

White, Jerry P., Paul S. Maxim and Dan Beavon, eds. (2003), *Aboriginal Conditions: Research as a Foundation for Public Policy* (Vancouver: UBC Press).

White-Harvey, Robert (1994), "Reservation Geography and the Restoration of Native Self-Government," *Dalhousie Law Journal* 17(2).

Wilkins, Kerry (1999), "But We Need the Eggs: The Royal Commission, the Charter of Rights and the Inherent Right of Aboriginal Self-Government," *University of Toronto Law Journal* 49 (1).

—— (2000), "Take Your Time and Do It Right: *Delgamuukw,* Self-Government Rights and the Pragmatics of Advocacy," *Manitoba Law Journal* 27 (2).

Williams, Melissa S. (2004), "Sharing the River: Aboriginal Representation in Canadian Political Institutions, in David Laycock, ed., *Representation and Democratic Theory* (Vancouver: UBC Press).

Windspeaker (2002), "All This Time and This is the Answer?" editorial. *Windspeaker* 20 (8).

—— (2003), "Sour Grapes: Lots of Wrath," editorial *Windspeaker*, 21 (8).

Wiwa, Ken (2001), "The Apostle of Forgiveness," *The Globe and Mail*, 5 May.

Wotherspoon, Terry (2003) "Prospects for a New Middle Class Among Urban Aboriginal Peoples" in Newhouse and Peters, eds., *Not Strangers in These Parts.*

York, Geoffrey and Loreen Pindera (1991), *People of the Pines: The Warriors and the Legacy of Oka* (Toronto: Little, Brown and Co.).

Queen's Policy Studies
Recent Publications

The Queen's Policy Studies Series is dedicated to the exploration of major policy issues that confront governments in Canada and other western nations. McGill-Queen's University Press is the exclusive world representative and distributor of books in the series.

School of Policy Studies

Global Networks and Local Linkages: The Paradox of Cluster Development in an Open Economy, David A. Wolfe and Matthew Lucas (eds.), 2005
Paper ISBN 1-55339-047-4 Cloth ISBN 1-55339-048-2

Choice of Force: Special Operations for Canada, David Last and Bernd Horn (eds.), 2005
Paper ISBN 1-55339-044-X Cloth ISBN 1-55339-045-8

Force of Choice: Perspectives on Special Operations, Bernd Horn, J. Paul de B. Taillon, and David Last (eds.), 2004   Paper ISBN 1-55339-042-3 Cloth ISBN 1-55339-043-1

New Missions, Old Problems, Douglas L. Bland, David Last, Franklin Pinch, and Alan Okros (eds.), 2004   Paper ISBN 1-55339-034-2 Cloth ISBN 1-55339-035-0

The North American Democratic Peace: Absence of War and Security Institution-Building in Canada-US Relations, 1867-1958, Stéphane Roussel, 2004
Paper ISBN 0-88911-937-6 Cloth ISBN 0-88911-932-2

Implementing Primary Care Reform: Barriers and Facilitators, Ruth Wilson, S.E.D. Shortt and John Dorland (eds.), 2004   Paper ISBN 1-55339-040-7 Cloth ISBN 1-55339-041-5

Social and Cultural Change, David Last, Franklin Pinch, Douglas L. Bland, and Alan Okros (eds.), 2004   Paper ISBN 1-55339-032-6 Cloth ISBN 1-55339-033-4

Clusters in a Cold Climate: Innovation Dynamics in a Diverse Economy, David A. Wolfe and Matthew Lucas (eds.), 2004   Paper ISBN 1-55339-038-5 Cloth ISBN 1-55339-039-3

Canada Without Armed Forces? Douglas L. Bland (ed.), 2004
Paper ISBN 1-55339-036-9 Cloth ISBN 1-55339-037-7

Campaigns for International Security: Canada's Defence Policy at the Turn of the Century, Douglas L. Bland and Sean M. Maloney, 2004
Paper ISBN 0-88911-962-7 Cloth ISBN 0-88911-964-3

Understanding Innovation in Canadian Industry, Fred Gault (ed.), 2003
Paper ISBN 1-55339-030-X Cloth ISBN 1-55339-031-8

Delicate Dances: Public Policy and the Nonprofit Sector, Kathy L. Brock (ed.), 2003
Paper ISBN 0-88911-953-8 Cloth ISBN 0-88911-955-4

Beyond the National Divide: Regional Dimensions of Industrial Relations, Mark Thompson, Joseph B. Rose and Anthony E. Smith (eds.), 2003
Paper ISBN 0-88911-963-5 Cloth ISBN 0-88911-965-1

The Nonprofit Sector in Interesting Times: Case Studies in a Changing Sector, Kathy L. Brock and Keith G. Banting (eds.), 2003
Paper ISBN 0-88911-941-4 Cloth ISBN 0-88911-943-0

Clusters Old and New: The Transition to a Knowledge Economy in Canada's Regions, David A. Wolfe (ed.), 2003 Paper ISBN 0-88911-959-7 Cloth ISBN 0-88911-961-9

The e-Connected World: Risks and Opportunities, Stephen Coleman (ed.), 2003 Paper ISBN 0-88911-945-7 Cloth ISBN 0-88911-947-3

John Deutsch Institute for the Study of Economic Policy

Current Directions in Financial Regulation, Frank Milne and Edwin H. Neave (eds.), Policy Forum Series no. 40, 2005   Paper ISBN 1-55339-072-5 Cloth ISBN 1-55339-071-7

Higher Education in Canada, Charles M. Beach, Robin W. Boadway and R. Marvin McInnis (eds.), 2005   Paper ISBN 1-55339-070-9 Cloth ISBN 1-55339-069-5

Financial Services and Public Policy, Christopher Waddell (ed.), 2004 Paper ISBN 1-55339-068-7 Cloth ISBN 1-55339-067-9

The 2003 Federal Budget: Conflicting Tensions, Charles M. Beach and Thomas A. Wilson (eds.), Policy Forum Series no. 39, 2004 Paper ISBN 0-88911-958-9 Cloth ISBN 0-88911-956-2

Canadian Immigration Policy for the 21st Century, Charles M. Beach, Alan G. Green and Jeffrey G. Reitz (eds.), 2003   Paper ISBN 0-88911-954-6 Cloth ISBN 0-88911-952-X

Framing Financial Structure in an Information Environment, Thomas J. Courchene and Edwin H. Neave (eds.), Policy Forum Series no. 38, 2003 Paper ISBN 0-88911-950-3 Cloth ISBN 0-88911-948-1

Available from: McGill-Queen's University Press
c/o Georgetown Terminal Warehouses
34 Armstrong Avenue
Georgetown, Ontario L7G 4R9
Tel: (877) 864-8477
Fax: (877) 864-4272
E-mail: orders@gtwcanada.com

See also publications from the Institute of Intergovernmental Relations.

Institute of Intergovernmental Relations
Recent Publications

Available from McGill-Queen's University Press:

Canadian Fiscal Federalism: What Works, What Might Work Better, Harvey Lazar (ed.), 2005
Paper ISBN 1-55339-012-1 Cloth ISBN 1-55339-013-X

Canada: The State of the Federation 2003, vol. 17, *Reconfiguring Aboriginal-State Relations,*
Michael Murphy (ed.), 2005   Paper ISBN 1-55339-010-5 Cloth ISBN 1-55339-011-3

Money, Politics and Health Care: Reconstructing the Federal-Provincial Partnership,
Harvey Lazar and France St-Hilaire (eds.), 2004
Paper ISBN 0-88645-200-7 Cloth ISBN 0-88645-208-2

Canada: The State of the Federation 2002, vol. 16, *Reconsidering the Institutions of
Canadian Federalism,* J. Peter Meekison, Hamish Telford and Harvey Lazar (eds.), 2004
Paper ISBN 1-55339-009-1 Cloth ISBN 1-55339-008-3

*Federalism and Labour Market Policy: Comparing Different Governance and Employment
Strategies,* Alain Noël (ed.), 2004   Paper ISBN 1-55339-006-7 Cloth ISBN 1-55339-007-5

The Impact of Global and Regional Integration on Federal Systems: A Comparative Analysis,
Harvey Lazar, Hamish Telford and Ronald L. Watts (eds.), 2003
Paper ISBN 1-55339-002-4 Cloth ISBN 1-55339-003-2

Canada: The State of the Federation 2001, vol. 15, *Canadian Political Culture(s) in
Transition,* Hamish Telford and Harvey Lazar (eds.), 2002
Paper ISBN 0-88911-863-9 Cloth ISBN 0-88911-851-5

Federalism, Democracy and Disability Policy in Canada, Alan Puttee (ed.), 2002
Paper ISBN 0-88911-855-8 Cloth ISBN 1-55339-001-6, ISBN 0-88911-845-0 (set)

Comparaison des régimes fédéraux, 2ᵉ éd., Ronald L. Watts, 2002   ISBN 1-55339-005-9

Health Policy and Federalism: A Comparative Perspective on Multi-Level Governance,
Keith G. Banting and Stan Corbett (eds.), 2002
Paper ISBN 0-88911-859-0 Cloth ISBN 1-55339-000-8

Comparing Federal Systems, 2nd ed., Ronald L. Watts, 1999   ISBN 0-88911-835-3

**The following publications are available from the Institute of Intergovernmental
Relations, Queen's University, Kingston, Ontario K7L 3N6
Tel: (613) 533-2080 / Fax: (613) 533-6868; E-mail: iigr@qsilver.queensu.ca**

First Nations and the Canadian State: In Search of Coexistence, Alan C. Cairns,
2002 Kenneth R. MacGregor Lecturer, 2005   ISBN 1-55339-014-8

Political Science and Federalism: Seven Decades of Scholarly Engagement, Richard Simeon,
2000 Kenneth R. MacGregor Lecturer, 2002   ISBN 1-55339-004-0

The Spending Power in Federal Systems: A Comparative Study, Ronald L. Watts, 1999
ISBN 0-88911-829-9

Étude comparative du pouvoir de dépenser dans d'autres régimes fédéraux, Ronald L. Watts,
1999   ISBN 0-88911-831-0

Working Paper Series

2005

1. *International Law and the Right of Indigenous Self-Determination: Should International Norms be Replicated in the Canadian Context?* by Jennifer E. Dalton

2. *Intergovernmental Fiscal Relations and the Soft Budget Constraint Problem* by Marianne Vigneault

3. *Property Taxation: Issues in Implementation* by Harry Kitchen

4. *The Impact of the Centralization of Revenues and Expenditures on Growth, Regional Inequality and Inequality* by Stuart Landon and Bradford G. Reid

5. *Autonomy or Dependence: Intergovernmental Financial Relations in Eleven Countries* by Ronald Watts

2004

1. *Should the Canadian Federation be Rebalanced?* by Robin Boadway

2. *The Changing Nature of Quebec-Canada Relations: From the 1980 Referendum to the Summit of the Canadas* by Thomas J. Courchene

3. *Financial Relationships between Regional and Municipal Authorities: Insights from the Examination of Five OECD Countries* by Melville L. McMillan

4. *Models of Government Structure at the Local Level* by Enid Slack

5. *Local Taxation in Selected Countries: A Comparative Examination* by Harry Kitchen

6. *Fiscal Federalism in Canada, the USA, and Germany – Final Report* by Robin Boadway and Ronald L. Watts

2005 Special Series on Asymmetric Federalism

(Posted on our website at http://www.iigr.ca under Research, then Browse Publications)

1. *Asymmetry in Canada, Past and Present* by David Milne

2. *Public Opinion On Asymmetrical Federalism: Growing Openness or Continuing Ambiguity?* by F. Leslie Seidle and Gina Bishop

3. *Some Asymmetries are More Legitimate than Others – And Subsidiarity Solves Most Things Anyway* by Gordon Gibson

4. *A Comparative Perspective on Asymmetry in Federations* by Ronald L. Watts

5. *Equality or Asymmetry? Alberta at the Crossroads* by F.L.(Ted) Morton

6. *The Case of Asymmetry in Canadian Federalism* by Jennifer Smith

7. *Speaking of Asymmetry. Canada and the 'Belgian Model'* by Andé Lecours

8. *The Historical and Legal Origins of Asymmetrical Federalism in Canada's Founding Debates: A Brief Interpretive Note* by Guy Laforest

9. *Beyond Recognition and Asymmetry* by Jocelyn Maclure

10. *The Scope and Limits of Asymmetry in Recent Social Policy Agreements* by Peter Graefe

11. *German Federalism – Still a Model of Symmetry?* by Saskia Jung

12. *Western Asymmetry* by Roger Gibbins

13. *Survivance versus Ambivalence: The Federal Dilemma in Canada* by Hamish Telford

For a complete list of Working Papers, see the Institute of Intergovernmental Relations web site at: www.iigr.ca. Working Papers can be downloaded from the web site under the pull down menu "Research."